MONTGOMERY COLLEGE LIBRARY
GERMANTOWN CAMPUS

WITHDRAWN

D1598466

ROOTS
OF A
REVOLUTION

ROOTS
OF A
REVOLUTION

Scenes from
Zimbabwe's Struggle

NDABANINGI SITHOLE

OXFORD LONDON NEW YORK
OXFORD UNIVERSITY PRESS
1977

Oxford University Press, Walton Street, Oxford OX2 6DP

OXFORD LONDON GLASGOW
NEW YORK TORONTO MELBOURNE WELLINGTON
IBADAN NAIROBI DAR ES SALAAM LUSAKA CAPE TOWN
KUALA LUMPUR SINGAPORE JAKARTA HONG KONG TOKYO
DELHI BOMBAY CALCUTTA MADRAS KARACHI

© *Ndabaningi Sithole* 1977

*All rights reserved. No part of this publication may be reproduced,
stored in a retrieval system, or transmitted, in any form or by any
means, electronic, mechanical, photocopying, recording, or otherwise
without the prior permission of Oxford University Press*

British Library Cataloguing in Publication Data

Sithole, Ndabaningi
  Roots of a Revolution.
  ISBN 0-19-215672-1
  I. Title
  823'.9'1F   PR9390.9.S/   77-30074

PRINTED AND BOUND IN ENGLAND BY
HAZELL WATSON AND VINEY LTD
AYLESBURY, BUCKS

I dedicate this work

> To all the Liberation Forces of Zimbabwe
> Who have fallen on the Battlefield
> Who have been sentenced to Death
> Who have been sentenced to Life Imprisonment
> Who have been condemned to Indefinite Detention
> And to Our Brave Men Carrying on the Struggle
> In the Noble Cause of the Liberation of the
>   Fatherland
> For which No Price is too High to Pay

Ndabaningi Sithole
28 March 1973

Contents

I

The 400

'Sons of the Soil!'

John Moyo was addressing a crowd of 400 men who had come to hear him and others as had been arranged.

Some had walked two miles to get to the meeting; some had walked five miles; some eight, and others ten. But others had been brought by car from as far afield as forty miles. The cars just dumped them by the roadside and died in the distance, while the men disappeared into the bush. The men were keen-eyed. They listened eagerly, no one coughed or laughed. No one smiled. No one talked. No one whispered. Everyone's eyes were fixed on the speaker. He was the man to tell them the things that troubled them; the things that had brought them there at this time of day. Even nature around them seemed to expect something from the speaker and from the meeting. The great, grey granite boulders rose to the sky as if standing to attention in honour of this occasion. The trees in heavy green foliage were silent with perfect stillness as if awaiting the message from John Moyo. The grass was dead still. Even the air seemed perfectly motionless. Man, tree, grass, rock, and air united in a perfect harmony of still-ness and silence, except for the speaker.

It was morning. The sun had risen only an hour or so ago, and it had some ten hours ahead of it to plough across the enormous blue sky before bidding everyone goodnight. The air in those mountains where the 400 had gathered was cool and calm, but the men's hearts were greatly agitated.

John Moyo, the main speaker, was in his early 40s. He

was a well educated man. He held a B.A. in political science, an M.A. in sociology, and a Ph.D. in anthropology. He was a lecturer at the local university, and was in receipt of a monthly salary of $300.00. He stood five feet nine inches in height, and his round head that was charmingly matched with his round brown face contained what the Western psychologists call a high I.Q. His skin was smooth and his teeth glistened when he smiled. Some men did not quite like it because they felt it tended to seduce their wives or their daughters. He had a most disarming smile for both men and women, and it sent the girls crazy. It was an ageless smile. But on this occasion, he had lost it altogether. He was serious, serious, and serious.

'Sons of the Soil,' said John Moyo, 'we are gathered here not as foreigners, but as Sons of the Soil, and yet we are gathered in this fearful and ignominious secrecy because of the foreigners who have taken our country and made it *theirs*.'

'Theirs!' thundered the 400. Some snarled, some cursed, some invoked the spirits of their ancestors to light upon the foreigners' heads.

'I say *theirs*,' continued John Moyo, 'not because it is *really* theirs, but because they say so, and because they treat us as strangers in the land of our birth. We, the Sons of the Soil, have become foreigners in our own country. Can you imagine that?'

'Absolutely unimaginable!' cried about a score of men.

'That's the price we pay for our unwillingness to fight like men,' a voice next to the speaker suggested.

'Fight!' roared the 400. 'Nothing else. Fight!'

A gentle breeze blew across the audience as if to calm their agitated feelings. The grass and the leaves rustled as if whispering approval. The great, grey granite rocks stood firm and erect as if trying to prevent these human voices from flying past them for security reasons. The glorious morning sun smiled upon the 400 as if to say: 'Good luck to you, Sons of the Soil!' The deep blue sky, looking down upon these black humans who had gathered together in the quest of their own rights, seemed to maintain a strict neutrality and aloofness far beyond their reach.

'We are met here, I repeat, not as foreigners but as Sons of the Soil,' John Moyo went on. 'Are there any foreigners among us here?'

'None! None!' roared the 400.

'We are met here not as money-lovers, but as Sons of the Soil. Are there any money-lovers here?'

'None! None!'

'We are met here not as European stooges or informers but as Sons of the Soil. Any European stooges or informers here?'

'None! None!'

'We are met here not as self-seekers, but as Sons of the Soil. Any self-seekers here?'

'None! None!'

'We are met here not as men who have been forced to come, but as Sons of the Soil. Anyone who has been forced to come here?'

'None! None!'

'We are met here as Sons of the Soil to open our hearts to one another. Am I right or wrong in this assumption?'

'Right!' they eagerly roared.

John Moyo paused and his quick eyes shot into theirs. For a full minute his eyes gazed into their souls, and the 400 looked at him without blinking as if to afford him the chance to see their souls, for indeed the soul of a man can be seen in his eyes. For that full minute the whole scene except for John Moyo was transfigured into solid human stillness and silence.

'Now I shall proceed to open my heart to you, Sons of the Soil,' said the speaker at length.

'Proceed, Son of the Soil,' the 400 begged him.

At this juncture some apparently frightened birds took to the sky and flew overhead. The flight had emerged from the east. Then another flight from the north, and just as the birds were almost directly above the 400 another flock of birds emerged from the south, so that the northern flock veered to the east while the southern one made directly for the north. Everyone silently watched the birds. Everyone seemed to know instinctively that these birds were heralding something. The birds had not flown with any appearance of leisure such as can be seen as they glide through the blue sky. They did not fly with any apparent ease. They were flapping away as if for dear life. Something must have frightened them, and they were trying frantically to outpace danger and to bring security nearer to themselves.

At this juncture three men emerged from the bush. One, coming from the east, said something into John Moyo's right ear and disappeared where he had emerged from. A second man, coming from the north side, did the same. Lastly, a third man appeared and had John Moyo's right ear all to himself for a minute or so, then disappeared back into the bush.

'It's clear,' said John Moyo; 'the foreigners are still having their tea, and we are having our meeting here.'

The 400 nodded their approval of the security arrangements John Moyo had apparently made prior to the meeting.

'It is now high time, Sons of the Soil,' began John Moyo, 'that we acted like men to retrieve our stolen land. We can no longer accept racial discrimination—*racial discrimination*—this evil that has poisoned every human value in this country, this venomous serpent which must be killed by any means. When the white man first came to this country, he said he discriminated against us because we wore animal skins. We now wear his clothes, but he continues to discriminate against us. He told us he discriminated against us because we were uneducated. We became educated, but he continues to discriminate against us. He told us he discriminated against us because we did not know his jobs. We now know them, but he continues to discriminate against us. He told us he discriminated against us because we were not Christian. We are now Christian, but he continues to discriminate against us. He told us he discriminated against us because we had not acquired his civilization. We have now acquired lots of it, but he continues to discriminate against us. For the last hundred years, we have been trying to follow the rules of the white man, but every time we satisfy these he deserts them, and creates new ones. He's not a man of his word. Can anyone here continue to believe in the word of the white man?'

'No!' roared the 400.

'Only a double fool,' remarked a voice.

'Only a fool multiplied by a hundred can continue to believe in the word of the white man,' said another voice.

'He's a liar!' half the audience cried.

'We were fools ever to believe him in the first place,' other voices cried in unison.

The 400 had become visibly agitated. John Moyo could feel the warmth of their souls. He could sense their deep anger and frustration.

'Can anyone tell me what racial discrimination means?' he asked, and without waiting for the answer he proceeded to answer the question himself: 'If a man discriminates against me because I am black, then he hates me. If he turns me out of a hotel because I am black, then he hates me. If he denies me access to public parks because I am black, then he hates me. If he denies me God's House because I am black, then he hates me. If a white government legislates against me because I am black then that government hates me. If I am paid low wages because I am black, then I am hated.

'You cannot discriminate against those you like. You cannot discriminate against those you love. You cannot discriminate against those you respect and hold in high esteem. You cannot discriminate against those you believe are your equals before the law and before God. Never! Never! You can only discriminate against those you dislike. Those you hate. Those you despise. Those you believe are your inferiors. Racial discrimination is a gospel of hatred pure and simple.

'No, Sons of the Soil, racial discrimination has no other meaning for me, for you, and for our people than that the white man hates the black man because the black man is black. He discriminates against the black man because he hates the black man. The fault of the black man in the eyes of the white man is that he is black. And now, white liberals tell us that we in turn should not hate the white man. Why not?'

'Hate him!' they roared with a fury that seemed to emanate from the very core of their being. 'Hate him! Hate him!'

'The white man in this country,' continued John Moyo, 'has created a system that rejects the black man because he is black. The white liberals now tell us to accept the white man because he is white. The price of rejection has to be acceptance! What folly! You accept a man who rejects you! Acceptance is equal to acceptance, and rejection to rejection. That's plain, isn't it? The white man rejects us and, therefore, we must reject him. It is sheer nonsense and the height of folly to say two wrongs cannot make one right. Remember, it takes two wars to produce peace! It is the white man who has started the war of racial hatred, and we must fight it with hatred. Wars are fought with wars. Make no mistake about that. I know war is no good for anyone, but it takes war to stop war. I know hatred is no good for anyone, but it takes hatred to stop hatred. This is the way of this world, and we are in it. Unless the white man stops his racial discrimination, we must fight him with it to make our point.'

The 400 cheered and cheered. It was not that kind of cheering stemming from superficiality, from cheap and gaudy sensation, from hypocrisy and blasphemy. No. It bordered on the holy. There was a human depth to it. Humanity and human tragedy rang deep and low in strains of fear and awe. The cheering stemmed from a deep sense of injustice. It stemmed from a profound appreciation that John Moyo had said exactly what the 400 had felt for so long a time, but lacked words to express. This was an occasion of soul speaking to soul, a soul-union consummated in common suffering. If those immortal grey granite rocks, those tall graceful trees, that freshly green grass, had had any souls of their own, they too would have shouted their unstinting approval, but, alas, man is man, and nature is nature, and nature will always remain indifferent to the causes of man however noble or ignoble.

John Moyo paused for a while, and keenly surveyed the targets of his oratory.

'What is the answer to this problem? For the last hundred years, we have prayed with these people. We have worked with these people. We have built towns and cities with these people. We have forced with our muscle-power the rock under the earth to yield its hidden treasure to these people. There is hardly anything we have not done with these people. We supply them with cheap labour. Without it most industries in this country would fold up. But what do we get in return for this co-operation? Racial discrimination, humiliating treatment. Third-rate citizenship. Less and poorer land. Low wages. We have become things at the disposal of these people. What is the answer to all these problems? Talk to the white man? We have done this for the last hundred years. Turn the other cheek? That also we have done for the last hundred years. Passive resistance? Trying to understand the white man? Both have failed for the last hundred years. Non-violence? That, too, has failed. Strikes? Demonstrations and protests? All these have failed. Everything else has hopelessly failed because white supremacy is a law unto itself. What then is the alternative left before us?'

'To fight!' roared the 400.

'With our tongues?'

'No!'

'With our pens?'

'No!'

'With conferences?'

'No!'

'With what, then?'

'Our very lives.'

'How?'

'Our blood must flow, their blood must flow.'

'No other alternative?'

'No. None! None! Blood! Blood! A hundred years is enough!'

'Do you realize what it means to fight?'

'It means we die, and the enemy dies. It means war.'

'And you know what war means?'

'It means the enemy extinguishes our life and we his.'

'It means blowing out the flame of life as we do to a candle,' added one young man.

'This is the necessary price we've to pay to be free in our own country,' said another.

'No man in his right mind wants to see bloodshed in this country,' observed one man whose head was mostly grey. 'But nor would any man in his right mind accept a political arrangement that makes him permanently the creature of the white man.'

'The white man regards the black man as a dog,' asserted one young radical with tears of anger flowing down his face.

'No,' contradicted another young radical; 'he treats us worse than a dog. There are public places in this country where dogs are allowed but where a black man is expressly forbidden.'

'You are right, Son of the Soil!' the 400 supported him.

'For instance,' went on the second young radical, 'if a white girl kisses me, she gets into trouble. I get into trouble. But if she kisses a dog she doesn't get into trouble. The dog does not get into trouble.'

'Leave that alone, Son of the Soil,' advised one old man. 'We are not here to consider the matter of their women. We are here to consider the affair of our soil.'

'Well spoken, Son of the Soil,' the 400 commended the old man. 'It's the soil, the soil, and our soil, not the women, the women, their women, but our soil. This is our soil, Sons of the Soil.'

Another old man spoke up: 'Until the foreigner gets it straight that we are quite prepared to kill and to be killed to reassert our stolen rights we are going nowhere. He'll never take us seriously. I know this is a terrible approach. But how else can we gain the independence that is rightly ours? Everything else has failed, and the white man here intends to hold the African in abject subjection indefinitely. We have, therefore, no other choice before us but to purchase our own independence with our very blood, and with theirs too!'

'That's right! That's right!' the 400 repeated.

'There's nothing else I need say to you, Sons of the Soil,' said John Moyo. 'At the beginning of this meeting I told you that we are here to open our hearts to one another. I have opened mine to you. Some of you have already spoken out. I'm sure more of you would like to.'

With these words he sat down on a flat rock, and another man rose to speak. He was Samuel Shava, a well-known advocate in the district and beyond it. He was, in fact, a national figure highly respected for his legal learning, and held in great affection for his identification with the common cause of the independence of Zimbabwe. He held an LL.B. and an LL.M. from the University of London and had successfully defended in court many African politicians, and had saved a few of them from the gallows. Samuel Shava stood six feet tall. In his late 30s, he was ebony black in complexion, imposing, massive, erect of posture, and broad-shouldered. His mind was totally preoccupied with the liberation of Zimbabwe. He had almost lost his appetite for women, and he had decidedly lost it for his beer. He had become a teetotaller. He, like others, had become a slave to the Great Cause which had taken many into captivity.

'I am not going to repeat. . . .' He stopped, and everyone looked in the eastern direction.

A man, the same man who had emerged from the same direction at the beginning of the meeting, came running up and shouted: '*Sango rachena!*—The bush is white!'

Everyone there seemed to know what that meant. Except for John Moyo, Samuel Shava, and three others, they all took off their coats and laid them down at various points not too far from their meeting-place. Four men dashed into the bush and emerged with four drums. One also sprang into the bush and brought back with him a black goat which he led by a rein. Five others disappeared in another direction and fetched five beer-pots full of *doro*—beer. These they placed in the open.

The four drummers began to play the drums, and the other Sons of the Soil began to sing and dance. Some whistled; some ululated; some clapped their hands and swayed their bodies; the song they all knew. The dance they also knew. Their fathers had sung it, they all also had danced to it to the accompaniment of the drums. The same thing was true of their forefathers and their forefathers' fathers and their forefathers. Enthusiastic singing, dancing, clapping, whistling, swaying soon rose to a fever pitch. But above this frenzy hung the ominous words: 'The bush is white!' They all knew what was coming, but they pretended to be only preoccupied with their singing and dancing.

John Moyo, Samuel Shava, and three others did not join in the singing and dancing of the rest of the Sons of the Soil. They had taken out their notebooks, and seemed to be observing and recording. They looked perfectly detached from the crowd, and perfectly composed on their rocks. They also knew that sooner or later the bush would be 'white'. But when?

Suddenly there emerged from the bush about forty police-men and soldiers with five Alsatian dogs on the leash. The whites were in the majority and the blacks in the minority. All these security forces were armed except for the blacks. Indeed, the bush had become 'white', but it had become more than that. It was now almost encircled with guns, and each gun was loaded with bullets, and each bullet contained a life-extinguisher! The security forces advanced towards the dancing crowd almost in a full circle, but not quite, and the Sons of the Soil took no notice of them. Captain Wood, who was in charge of the operation, went towards John Moyo.

'Good morning, Dr Moyo,' he greeted him.

'Good morning to you, Captain Wood,' reciprocated John Moyo.

'How are you this fine morning?'

'Quite well, thank you, and how are you?'

'Fine, thanks.'

A short period of uneasy silence followed between the two men.

'What's all this? It looks most interesting,' said Captain Wood at length.

'It's ancestral intercession, just at the beginning of it,' explained John Moyo.

'I see. What's that black goat for?'

'For this ancestral occasion,' John Moyo replied. 'We have four more.'

'I see. What's that beer for?'

'For the same thing.'

'But why should a man like you be here?'

'My main field of interest is anthropology, and I have been taking notes since this morning,' said John Moyo. 'I couldn't let this chance pass by.'

Then he showed Captain Wood some of the notes ostensibly taken that morning. 'Karanga ancestral worship is most fascinating.'

Insatiable curiosity had practically seized all the security forces. The drums echoed in their souls if they had any. The song poured into their ears and loosened some of their official reserve and aloofness. The dance caused them to sway their uniformed and armed bodies. They glued their eyes on the singers, dancers, and drummers, and forgot that they were security men.

'What surprises me, Dr Moyo, and the white man in general,' resumed Captain Wood, 'is that in spite of Western civilization, these educated men still follow these heathen practices. We can't understand that. Many of these fellows are educated, aren't they?'

'More than half of them are,' said John Moyo.

'You see!' cried Captain Wood. 'And how can we have equal rights under such circumstances?'

John Moyo made no comment. He wanted to give Captain

Wood the impression that he was in agreement with him. Almost all whites seem to believe that silence implies consent. But John Moyo's was merely a tactical silence. It would have been highly impolitic to start a political argument with Captain Wood, who was looking for evidence of a political gathering for prosecution.

The dancers stopped for a while. A *nganga*—witchdoctor—took a gourdful of beer and poured it on the black goat's head and chanted a few words to the accompaniment of clapping of hands according to a certain rhythmic pattern, and in this John Moyo and the four others joined. After this, for the first time, the people looked casually at the security men.

'Hey, men, come here and sit down and drink some beer with us,' called Chomudondo, who was always forward.

The security men looked at one another in surprise. They had not expected such an invitation. Even Captain Wood, their commander, was somewhat taken aback.

'No!' objected one clown among the 400. 'They must not drink our beer. They'll get drunk and start shooting one another.'

Laughter broke out on both sides. It held a genuine hilarity, although, ironically, the whites were full of racial discrimination in their hearts, while the blacks were overflowing with hate. But this laughter, added to the ancestral song and dance, the black goat, the five beer-pots, and John Moyo's 'anthropological notes', helped Captain Wood to label the gathering officially as 'religious and non-political'.

Twenty minutes after the departure of all the security men, another man came running, and announced, '*Sango ranaka*—the bush is clear.' Then drums stopped, then the singing and the dancing. Everyone sat down, thoroughly satisfied that they had put off the security forces who had been informed by some black spy that John Moyo was going to hold an illegal political meeting on that day and at this place. The black spy had been discredited! It was some time before everyone could be quieted down: success is always exciting.

'I was about to say that I was not going to repeat what the Son of the Soil had just said,' resumed Samuel Shava. 'I agree with every word that he said. He has spoken my heart. But I want to add something so that you can also see what more is in my heart.'

He looked around at the 400, now quiet and attentive.

'Sons of the Soil!' Samuel Shava began. 'It is a great shame that we are not independent. A great shame indeed! A shame to us! A shame to our children! A shame to our children's children! A great shame indeed!'

'A great shame indeed!' thundered the 400.

'Our black brothers to the north of us are independent, but we are not,' he said. 'Do you know what black countries are now independent or not independent?'

'Yes, we do!'

'Zambia?' he cried in holy indignation.

'Independent.'

'Malawi?'

'Independent.'

'Botswana?'

'Independent.'

'Tanzania?'

'Independent.'

'Kenya?'

'Independent.'

'Uganda?'

'Independent.'

'Zaïre?'

'Independent.'

'Nigeria?'

'Independent.'

'Ghana?'

'Independent.'

'Zimbabwe?'

'Not independent.'

'Why not?' he posed the question.

His bloodshot eyes darted from side to side as if accusing

the 400 of non-independence. The causes of non-independence they all knew, but they ran short of words. Speech seemed to have taken wings and flown away from them. They fully realized that all these countries had been under the rule of the white man for a long time, but the black man there had won his independence all the same. The black man in Zimbabwe had not won it. Why? Why? Why? This was the question. It was not because of the white man that they had not won their independence, but it was because of the black man in Zimbabwe. Elsewhere independence had been won in spite of, and not because of, the white man. The independence they were seeking had to be won from the white man, and it had to be won by themselves. They were their own liberators. That was what Samuel Shava was trying to get them to see.

'Why haven't we got independence here?' He reiterated the question. 'Are people in these countries not black like ourselves?'

'They are,' answered the 400.

'Were they not under the thumb of the white man as we are today?' Samuel Shava asked with consuming eyes.

'They were.'

'Did the people in Kenya not suffer before they got their independence?'

'They did.'

'Did people in Algeria not suffer before they got their independence?'

'They did.'

'The birth of independence, like the birth of a human being, entails suffering. We must learn to suffer for ourselves, to suffer for our children, and to suffer for their children's children. Better to die liberating Zimbabwe than to die by natural processes. We have no other alternative but to fight and fight and fight!'

'Fight! Fight! Fight!' responded the 400, shaking their fists in the air.

'What do you think our black brothers to the north think

of us when we seem unable to win our independence as they did theirs? Do you think they respect us for this?'

'No! They despise us.'

'We've become Africa's laughing-stock. We've become the world's laughing-stock. And we deserve it. There is only one thing for cowards. Contempt! Contempt! Contempt! That's all they deserve. We have no alternative but to become independent by any means.'

'Hear, hear, Son of the Soil,' they applauded.

Samuel Shava sat down, and then a 55-year-old chief stood up to open his heart also. He was Chief Joseph Shumba, a man of grave disposition. He lacked the devilish eloquence of either John Moyo or Samuel Shava, their hyperbole so necessary in subversive activities, their oratorical exuberance so necessary in carrying away a fear-ridden people, their sense of the dramatic, and the many advantages of their formal and higher education; but the cause of Zimbabwe was deep down in his heart. It was not difficult for him, therefore, to speak. The deep cause loosens the tongue and sets it on the high road of political oratory. The depth of the spirit is the very height of speech. Here stood the old aristocratic chief in whose heart African grievances against the white man had accumulated for 55 years!

'Now, Sons of the Soil,' he began. 'You are talking in the language I understand; the language that my forefathers understood; the language that their fathers also understood.'

The old chief here posed with his chiefly chin held in the air, as if deliberately seeking to cause the 400 to listen more attentively.

'Fighting is a bad thing,' he declared, 'but to refuse to fight when you are treated like a dog is worse.'

'Right! Right!' the 400 concurred.

'In this world,' he went on, 'there are two ways of fighting. You fight with your tongue. That's the first one. You fight with weapons. That's the second one. If the tongue fails, weapons step in. If weapons fail, the tongue steps in. It goes like this: tongue, weapon. Weapon, tongue. Tongue, weapon. Weapon, tongue. Is this the occasion for the tongue?'

'No!' the 400 enthusiastically negatived.

'What's the occasion then?' he demanded.

'Weapons!' they roared back.

'And that means . . . ?' he asked.

'Fighting!' they answered.

'That's right. That's my heart, Sons of the Soil.' And with these words he sat down in the midst of prolonged cheers and applause. The 400 were clearly on fire. They had seen his heart. They had caught its warmth and sincerity. The old chief had lent tremendous weight to the cause of the Sons of the Soil.

There were more speakers who opened their hearts after this, but whatever they said there was only one theme, that there was to be no compromise with white domination. It had to be dealt a deathblow. The 400 were unanimous on drastic action against subjection.

The glorious sun which had been laboriously ploughing across the vast blue deep for the whole day had now only about an hour or so to go before sinking behind the western range of mountains, and before bidding everyone good-night. The cool breezes of the evening gently blew over the green bush as if trying to calm the greatly agitated feelings of the people gathered there. The green grass and the heavy foliage quietly rustled as if to hush the 400, for the matter in their hearts was grave and clearly needed more time and care. Under the benediction of the vast blue void, the 400 stood at attention and sang their national anthem and then dispersed to their various destinations supercharged with a new evangelical zeal for the liberation of Zimbabwe.

If the reader is to appreciate fully the intensity and extensity of involvement and commitment of the 401, it is as well to explain certain facts.

Who were 'the Sons of the Soil'? Were they only 401? Were they only male? Were they only adults? Were they

only Zimbabweans? Were they a special clan or tribe? The
answer is of course a negative one.

'Sons of the Soil' is an English translation of the Shona
phrase '*Vana Vevu*' which literally means 'Children of the
Soil'. Since at this meeting there were only men and no
women I gave preference to a rather arbitrary translation
over the literal version. This is the first reason. The second
reason is that to a Shona ear '*Vana Vevu*'—'Children of the
Soil'—was not offensive. Even men in their 70s cheerfully
regarded themselves as 'Children of the Soil'. There was
nothing derogatory about it. '*Vana Vevu*' had a special appeal
to both young and old, male and female. It was ageless. It
was sexless. Both young and old, both male and female, were
and are of the Soil. '*Vana Vevu*' was a salutation loaded with
deep and stirring emotion.

Let no foreigner rush to the conclusion that these people
felt they were literally children; that they felt weak and help-
less; that they were looking for a father to fight their battles
for them. No. Far from it. Woe unto that foreigner who
would have called to them: 'Children, children, come here.'
Even the people of Zimbabwe themselves didn't call themselves in that fashion. They dared not address one another as
'Children' but always as 'Children of the Soil'. If anyone had
addressed the 400 simply as 'Children' this would have been
offensive. It would have jarred against their feelings. It would
have been in poor taste, and highly improper. It would have
been simply one of those things which were never done. Con-
vention would have frowned. Good manners would have
gently disapproved. Propriety would have protested. Reason
would have criticized. Dignity would have been insulted.

But of course '*Vana Vevu*', 'Children of the Soil', was more
than a designation for all the black people of Zimbabwe. It
was a clarion call to all those who were denied their full
rights and freedoms in their own native land. It was a rally-
ing-point. It was political through and through. It had
political nuances that aroused the deep emotions of the black
man against the Nordic nonsense which in Rhodesia went

under the appellation 'white supremacy'. 'Children of the Soil' meant the downtrodden black man—downtrodden by the white man. But it was never a doctrine of self-pity. Never a philosophy of pessimism or doom. Never a theory of passiveness. Never a programme of withdrawal. It was a political doctrine of self-realization, of self-assertion, of determination, of hope, of resolve to be free of the heavy yoke of white supremacy which the white man fastened on the necks of all the blacks of Zimbabwe nearly a hundred years ago. Hence *Vana Vevu* carried with it the militant message: 'Sons of the Soil! Arise and fight!' To divorce it from its militancy, or its militancy from it, would be to miss its true meaning and relevance.

But *Vana Vevu* was more than a political reality. It was philosophical as well. Was it *Vana Vevu* or also *Vu reVana*? Was it 'Children of the Soil' or also 'The Soil of the Children'?

It was not a question of either/or. It was both.

The black man belonged to the Soil. It claimed him. He and millions of others to come belonged to the Soil which had given birth to millions of his kind stretching back well beyond the human memory and lost in antiquity. The Soil had given birth to thousands of thousands of generations and it had received them back into its bosom after their sojourn on earth. The black man belonged to the Soil by right of birth. He belonged to it by right of death as well. To deprive him of it was to rob him of his birth-right and his death-right! The Soil possessed him by right of his many ancestors who had lived on it and who had been buried in it. The Soil gave him life, and when that life left him, it claimed him back. He came from it and therefore he belonged to it. No one comes from where he does not belong. At death he returned to it. No one returns where he does not belong. He is of the Soil in life and death—*'Mwana we Vu'*, 'Child of the Soil'.

But it was not only the Soil that possessed the black man, but he, the black man, also possessed it. It was his as much as he was of the Soil. He tilled it to sustain his life. He exploited it in other ways for his own benefit. It supported him. It was his servant, and in a similar capacity it had served countless generations before him, and it would serve countless generations after him. He stood between the long past and the long future guilty before the dead and the unborn that he had allowed this Soil—this God-given Substance of Life—to pass into the grasping hand of the foreigner.

'Children of the Soil' therefore meant those who were possessed by the Soil, and those who possessed it. But under foreign rule the black man lost possession of the Soil. It passed to the foreigner. To retrieve this lost possession was the black man's Problem Number One. The black man's hatred of the white man stemmed from this fact, and the white man's fear of the black man had its origin in the same thing.

But to return to the 401. Who were they?

They were the land-dispossessed black men of Zimbabwe. But the dispossession did not end there. They were dispossessed of their human dignity; dispossessed of fundamental human rights; dispossessed of basic human freedoms; dispossessed of the franchise; dispossessed of human equality; dispossessed of equality before the law; dispossessed of equal opportunities; dispossessed of self-determination in the land of their birth. Their children were dispossessed well in advance long before they were born. They would arrive in this world to find themselves dispossessed all round. They would grow up in dispossession, spend their childhood in dispossession, spend their adulthood in dispossession, grey and die in dispossession, and finally be buried in dispossession. This was the sharp sting of being a dispossessed people. Who had so effectively dispossessed the six million blacks represented by these 401 black men? The white man. What right had a few white men numbering less than a quarter of a million to dispossess six million blacks? Might. As simple as all that. Democracy? No. Civilization? No. Education? No. Might, might, might, and there ended the matter. 'Might is right' was the white man's motto, and 'Right is might' his studied hypocrisy to conceal the truth of his inferiorizing rule.

That the 401 happened to be only male was due to the secret nature of the meeting. The men did not like to involve the women. They knew very well that the course of action on which they were about to embark was a dangerous one. It was likely to have serious consequences and if the women kept out of it, so much the better for the children and for the womenfolk themselves.

The composition of the 401 will give the reader a good picture of the intensity and extensity of the involvement and commitment of the Sons of the Soil.

They ranged in age from 20 to 65 years. They included teachers, preachers, clerks, storekeepers, drivers, farmers, peasants, male nurses, policemen, soldiers, prison warders, agricultural demonstrators, dip attendants, medicine men. They were of many churches and religious persuasions. There were Roman Catholics, Anglicans, Methodists, followers of the Dutch Reformed Church, the United Church of Christ, the Zionist Church, the Apostolic Church, and there were, in addition, many who followed their traditional religion. Their education? There were illiterates and university graduates, and some at every educational level between the two. There were unmarried men, monogamists, and polygamists, so together with their wives and children the 401 represented a hundred different clans and ten different tribes.

Thus, the Great Cause appealed to all ages. While the Sons of the Soil belonged to different age-groups almost incompatible at first sight, it generated a we-feeling that clearly transcended age. The Great Cause cut across all professions, trades, and other occupations. Occupational prejudice gave way in the face of the common enemy—white supremacy—that product of diseased human minds which had poisoned all human relations, turned them sour and bitter so that black and white though sharing a common territory and a common history were worlds apart, and between them was a solid wall of fear, impregnable and terrible. The Great

Cause pulled down all religious barriers, and people learned
to think of themselves first as Sons of the Soil rather than
as members of this or that religious denomination. Their religious causes became subordinated to the Great Cause. The
Great Cause eliminated all educational differences. Intel-
lectual snobbery receded into the background in shame and
in fear of the Cause which demanded higher and more last-
ing values than the mere pretensions of high learning. And
the Great Cause appealed to the married and unmarried
men alike, to monogamists and polygamists the same, and
similarly, to divergent families, clans, and tribes. Clan and
tribal differences were buried, never to breathe any more
confusion among the Children of the Soil throughout the
land, and on their graves grew that charmed and bewitching
invisible Reality—'Sons of the Soil'.

2

The Evening of Miracles

'You know, according to Tom Dawson, not one of the white men we'll see tonight has ever heard an educated African speak,' said John Moyo to his friend Samuel Shava. 'When Mr Dawson told one of them that Dr Moyo was coming to speak to them, he said: "That's exciting. I've never met a witchdoctor before. Is this one the best of the witchdoctors?"'

Both men laughed heartily at the ignorance of the white man. They were driving in a small blue Volkswagen from Highfields to Tom Dawson's farm some miles outside Salisbury. It was to be a private meeting attended by about thirty European men only.

'It should be quite a meeting tonight,' said Samuel Shava, as the car pulled up in front of a large, handsome house. 'I hope they won't blame your speech on poor Dawson.'

'Why should they?' John Moyo asked.

'Well, every white liberal is supposed to teach every black man how to toe the line . . .,' said Samuel Shava.

'Good evening, John. Good evening, Mr Shava,' called their host, coming eagerly forward from his front door to greet them. 'I'm so glad you came.'

Tom Dawson literally lit up with joy. He had been anxious whether John Moyo would make it on time. The black man as a rule was notorious for lack of punctuality. Even if he had a wristwatch on or a pocket watch he nearly always failed to keep time. If John Moyo had arrived late Dawson feared that the white men gathered at his house would have proved their point against the black. He therefore sighed with great relief that John Moyo had arrived ten minutes before time!

The white man is universally a creature of time. Keeping time is one of his great virtues. But the black man is universally a timeless creature. Keeping no time although he may have an expensive watch is one of his great vices. But John Moyo was an exception to the rule. To arrive late for any appointment was almost a criminal offence with him.

Dawson showed the two black gentlemen into the living room where twenty-seven white gentlemen were seated around. They all stood up, and Dawson introduced John Moyo first. They all bowed stiffly and so did John Moyo in acknowledgement. Then John Moyo introduced his friend Samuel Shava, and the mention of his title, 'Advocate', melted away some of their stiffness and lit up their eyes with curiosity. There was a visible stir across the room. Ceremony over, the thirty men took their seats in great anticipation.

To one who does not know the true nature of a society that is based on the philosophy of white supremacy, nothing spectacular had taken place up to this point, but to the one who knows such a society miracles had already happened.

The first miracle was that twenty-seven whites had gathered there to hear a black man talk to them, to be the target of black oratory, to hear a black man put forward his point of view. To concede that the black man had something worthwhile to say to the white man was a big achievement in itself.

The second miracle was that John Moyo's car had stopped right in front of Tom Dawson's house just as any European visitor's would have done. African cars were supposed to park away from the residence of the white man, and then the black man would walk up to the house. Parking in front of Dawson's house was regarded as social equality and this had to be avoided at all cost. But that night it happened, and Dawson had insisted on it.

The third miracle was that John Moyo and Samuel Shava

were ushered in through the front door! This was an open violation of white supremacy. The custom of the white man screamed against it. It was one of those things that ought not to be done under any circumstances.

The fourth miracle was that the twenty-seven white gentlemen stood up when these two black gentlemen entered the house and bowed in stiff politeness when they were introduced to them! This looked like a topsy-turvy world where a white man stands up to acknowledge the arriving presence of a black man! White supremacy must have felt deeply offended that night. But more miracles were yet to take place.

It was difficult to tell what kind of response John Moyo would receive. There were two or three of them who had clean hungry looks with an icy aloofness bordering on resentfulness. Two screwed their faces—whether out of habit or because of this unusual evening, it was difficult to tell. A handful did not look at the two black gentlemen. Whether it was out of good manners or it needled their eyes to behold two black gentlemen instead of an African cook, this was also hard to tell. One or two appeared cynical, while about three seemed amused. But there were a few friendly faces, and a generous sprinkling of indifferent ones.

'It's about time now,' said Tom Dawson, looking at his wristwatch, and everyone looked at his.

Dawson briefly introduced John Moyo. He referred to their friendship extending over ten years, and mentioned the fact that the gentlemen gathered there were all interested in the future of the country, which depended on the co-operation of both black and white.

Then John Moyo rose. He thanked Mr Dawson for the trouble he had taken in arranging for the meeting, and thanked the white gentlemen for the trouble they had taken to attend it.

For the next twenty-five minutes he dwelt on the problems facing the country. He pointed out the bankruptcy of the policy of white supremacy, its failure over the last hundred years, its responsibility for the present tension between black and white, and ended by saying, 'Black and white are here to live together. That is self-evident. The question, however, is: how are they to live together? White supremacy demands that they live together on the basis that Europeans remain high and Africans low, regardless of everything else. The result is racial tension, hate and fear with violence clearly written on the sky, and only those who have the constitutional power can avert the obvious danger.'

The white gentlemen had been impressed by and large, but they subjected him to a volley of searching questions.

John Brown, who had been listening very intently, started the ball rolling. 'Dr Moyo,' he said, 'do you believe in violence?'

'It all depends upon what you mean.'

'I mean political violence.'

'It's difficult to say yes or no.'

A stir ran through the assembly.

'Why?' insisted Brown.

'Because there are two kinds of violence. I don't know which you have in mind.'

Another stir ran through the assembly. The white gentlemen sat back and looked at him more keenly.

'There are destructive violence and redemptive violence.'

'What's that, Dr Moyo?'

'Destructive violence is wanton violence.'

'For example?'

'When Adolf Hitler unleashed indiscriminate aggression, and wantonly exterminated six million Jews, four million Germans, and two-and-a-half-million other nationals, this was destructive violence.'

'And redemptive violence, as you call it?'

'This is violence to protect or preserve or redeem.'

'For example?'

'When the Allied forces, for instance, unleashed violence against the Nazi forces by air, land, and sea, this was redemptive or protective violence.'

'In other words, Dr Moyo, you believe in bloodshed?'

'In wanton bloodshed, no, in redemptive bloodshed, yes.'

The white audience fastened their eyes on John Moyo.

'It doesn't sound quite right to me.'

'Well, you'll no doubt appreciate that the principle of re-demptive bloodshed has preserved the sovereignty of many nations throughout the ages. All nations accept it. To re-pudiate it would be to repudiate national survival. Some have to die, if needs be, to save others. This is what I mean by redemptive bloodshed.'

'It's a costly principle.'

'I agree, but this is nearly always the last resort when everything else has failed. Most people want to stay alive if they can, but there comes a time in a people's life when they must decide to reassert their human dignity by implementing this principle as a last resort to drive their point home.'

The next questioner was Stanley Moore, who seemed to have been thinking deeply all this time. 'Dr Moyo,' he said, 'I wish to take you up on one point.'

'Yes?'

'You talk of redemptive violence. What exactly is to be redeemed by violence?'

'Taking our situation here as a good case in point, violence is supposed to redeem the black man from the injustices of white supremacy.'

'What injustices, for example?'

'Injustices created by job reservations on racial grounds, by racial discrimination in public places, by an economy that is deliberately depressed against the black man, by a qualified franchise that disqualifies most African adults from voting but which enfranchises most European adults, and by a political set-up which treats black people as third-rate citizens in the land of their birth.'

'But surely this can be put right by constitutional means?'

'Only the white man in this country has those means.'

'So you feel violence is necessary to put these things right?'

'That's not the point at issue.'

'What is the point?'

'The point is that suppose the African people turned to violence as a last resort, this would be redemptive violence.'

Robert Hatfield was the next to brainpick him. Looking straight into his face he asked: 'Have you visited any of the Communist countries?'

'Oh yes, quite a good number.'

A visible shudder ran through the assembly. The mere admission that he had visited Communist countries troubled them. Now they saw before them a live Communist, so they thought.

'What countries?'

'The Soviet Union, the People's Republic of China, North Korea, and a few others.'

'Yugoslavia?'

'Yes, that too.'

'Hungary?'

'Yes.'

'Bulgaria?'

'Yes.'

'It sounds as if you have visited every Communist country.'

'Not quite.'

'And Cuba?'

'Oh yes. That too.'

Horror sat on the faces of the white gentlemen. Their eyes became wider with more wonder. Their mouths remained open with surprise. What were they to make of it?

'But remember,' cautioned Moyo, 'I have also visited the U.S.A., Canada, Britain, France, Holland, and the Scandinavian countries.'

The white gentlemen heaved a sigh of uneasy relief.

'But why visit all these Communist countries?'

'Why not?'

Virtually all the white gentlemen came down with laughter.

'I suppose your next question will be why I visited these Western countries!'

Again the white gentlemen laughed. But the question was never asked.

'Are you, Dr Moyo, a Communist?'

'I am a Zimbabweanist.'

'Not a Communist?'

'No, of course not.'

'What do you mean by a Zimbabweanist?'

'I am a man who is dedicated to the cause of the people of Zimbabwe, not Communism.'

'Ah, but African nationalism here is Communist-inspired,' objected Hatfield with a great deal of feeling.

'That's incorrect!'

'But it is!' about half the white men cried in protest.

'Communism is outside this country, but African nationalism here is inspired by white supremacy inside this country.'

'Oh no!' they shouted in unison.

'In 1893, I'm sure you remember the Ndebeles rose against the whites. Was there Communism then? Of course not! In 1896 and 1897 the Ndebele and Shona respectively rebelled against the whites here. Was there Communism then? From 1900 to 1903 there was Mapondera's rebellion in this country. Was there Communism then? But note carefully that white supremacy began in this country in 1890 and has continued up to this day. What inspires African nationalism is the condition of white supremacy. You cannot run away from this historical fact.'

'But,' strenuously objected Hatfield, 'the so-called African freedom fighters are Communist-trained and armed with Communist weapons.'

'But,' countered John Moyo, 'to be Communist-trained is not one and the same thing as to be Communist-inspired. Nor is to be equipped with Communist arms the same thing as to be Communist-inspired.'

'You are now quibbling with words, Dr Moyo.'

'Not at all. To say that African nationalism is Communist-inspired is to suggest that it is caused by Communism, which it is not. It is caused by conditions prevailing here, and not outside this country. To say that African freedom fighters are equipped with Communist weapons to come and fight in this country, and therefore African nationalism is Communist-inspired, is a gross distortion of fact. After all, the Communists are already independent. It is the African who is not independent who is fighting. What inspires African nationalism here is the very fact that the African people are not independent. Communism comes to their aid only at their invitation, and who wouldn't welcome practical help to liberate themselves? If you good gentlemen were in our position, you would cheerfully accept Communist help.'

'Oh no,' some tried to laugh off the suggestion.

'Oh yes,' insisted John Moyo. 'Remember what happened during the last world war?'

'What was that?' innocently asked Hatfield.

'The British, the Americans, and the French fought side by side with Communist forces to defeat Nazism. The African may have to fight side by side with the same forces to defeat white supremacy.'

The white gentlemen sat back as if trying to take a fresh look at him. They apparently disliked his argument, but it was unassailable.

Gilbert Edwards was the next to fire a question at John Moyo. 'There's so much talk these days about Black Power. Not only in this country but in America as well. What really is it?' he asked.

'You are right, sir,' John Moyo began, 'that Black Power is also to be found in America just as it is to be found here.'

'And in South Africa,' called out a voice.

'Quite,' concurred John Moyo.

'Why?' asked Edwards.

'Black Power,' John Moyo said, 'is to be found wherever the black man is discriminated against as a racial group.'

The white gentlemen listened more keenly and looked at him more earnestly as if trying hard to read his mind.

'In one sense Black Power is a protest against racial discrimination,' explained John Moyo.

'But it's more than that, it seems to me,' remarked Edwards.

'You are right. It's a militant protest against racial discrimination.'

'That's where the danger lies—the militancy of Black Power,' chipped in a man called Jonathan Radley. 'The young blacks are up in arms against the white man everywhere.'

'Not quite,' corrected John Moyo. 'The young blacks are indeed up in arms, but not against the white man.'

'But against whom?' Radley asked, unable to contain himself. 'Against whom? Against whom?'

'Not against any particular person or group of persons.'

'Oh, come on now, Dr Moyo,' objected Radley. 'Everyone knows that Black Power is against white people as white people.'

'You're quite wrong, I'm afraid,' insisted John Moyo.

The white men looked amazed. Here was a black man telling one of them that he was wrong! This black man had risen above the station of a black man! White gentlemen were not used to being told by a black man that they were quite wrong even where they themselves knew they were wrong. But they maintained a stony silence and waited to hear what he was going to say by way of correcting the white man.

'You see,' said John Moyo, 'Black Power is against a system of racial discrimination, not against the white man. For instance, Black Power in this country is against white supremacy, not against white people as white people. I am dead against white supremacy, but I'm not dead against you. The British, for instance, were dead against Nazism, but were not against the Germans.'

'I think you've made your point, Dr Moyo,' one Ian Bell acknowledged.

'To come back to Mr Edwards's question "What is Black Power?", I wanted to say that it is a militant reassertion of the black man wherever he is racially discriminated against.

Black Power will spend itself in proportion to waning racial discrimination against the black man. The removal of racial discrimination is its natural grave.'

'The time is moving very fast tonight,' said Ian Bell, looking at his watch. 'But I must admit this is one of the most fascinating evenings I've had for years. I wish, however, to make a few observations to our distinguished speaker, and invite his comments. Dr Moyo, you'll appreciate that before the white man set foot here there was not a single town. Everything was bush, bush.'

'I do,' nodded Moyo.

'Because everything was bush, bush,' went on Bell, 'lions ate a lot of your people in this country.'

'Quite so,' John Moyo agreed.

'You'll no doubt remember that your people walked almost naked before the whites came, but now they put on the same clothes as we do. You yourselves bear witness to this fact.'

'About that there can be no doubt.'

'Now the white man has brought you beautiful towns and cities, schools, better transport and communication. You have better medical facilities. You can earn money which you never did before the white man came here.

'But it seems to me that the black man is quite ungrateful to the white man who has done all these things for him. Now he wants to have the white man thrown out of the country. This is the typical ingratitude of. . . .'

He almost said 'savages' but discretion prevailed.

John Moyo's eyes twinkled.

'With regard to your stopping the lions from eating us as a result of your establishing towns and cities in this country, I'm sure, Mr Bell, you'll appreciate that your cars eat more of my people every year than lions ever did before the white man came,' John Moyo said.

The white gentlemen looked at one another in amused surprise. Never before had they realized that in introducing the car into Rhodesia, they had introduced something more dangerous than a lion in point of human life.

'But with regard to the other things that the white man brought to this country,' continued John Moyo, 'I have nothing to add or subtract except to say this. The fact that the white man introduced these is neither here nor there.'

The white gentlemen looked at him more closely. Wasn't he grateful to the white man for all these things?

'We have a Shona proverb which says, "What was eaten long ago cannot satisfy the child," ' said Moyo. 'That is to say, you cannot solve the problems of today by applying solutions of long ago. Too often the white man in the 1970s tends, in his own mind, to deal with the African in the 1890s instead of the African of the 1970s! The African of today demands independence, never mind what your forefathers brought to our forefathers. Let us face the present and not escape into the past to avoid our present-day problems.'

'Oh, but the past is important,' Bell pointed out.

'For the dead, yes. For the living, no.'

'Oh no, . . .' said Bell, shaking his head.

'You see, Mr Bell, the fault with the white man in this country is that he refuses to deal with the present African. He pines for the dead African who used to tremble before his forefathers. But the novelty of the white man has had its day.'

'Perhaps you have a point there,' Bell grudgingly conceded.

'I think we are all agreed, or we should be agreed, that the past is for the dead, the future for the unborn, and the present for the living. Since all of us are alive, let us face squarely the problems of the living.'

There were more questions and answers on socialism, land apportionment, the inefficiency of the African, his rural mentality which made him dead wood in industrial development, African population explosion, African education, and the like.

'It's exactly ten o'clock,' said Tom Dawson at last.

'The time went very fast tonight,' observed Stanley Moore. Tom Dawson formally thanked John Moyo for his talk, and everyone applauded enthusiastically. They stood up to stretch and one by one went up to John Moyo and shook hands with him and thanked him. 'Splendid job,' 'Come again,' 'You sure opened my eyes, Dr Moyo,' were among the compliments paid him. Everyone felt the meeting had been worth while. Tea was served and lively discussion continued.

The fifth miracle that evening was that the white gentlemen were willing to exchange ideas and views with a black man, who was often regarded as incapable of thought, and that in some of the heated arguments no white gentleman had walked out of the meeting in disgust and to teach the black man his place!

The sixth miracle was that throughout the two-hour meeting a good number referred to John Moyo properly as Dr Moyo. It usually took real effort for a white man to do that. But that evening it seemed almost natural. Some referred to him as 'our distinguished guest' and not even the distinguished guest. A we-feeling had clearly developed, for it would be impossible to say 'our' in the absence of this. The white gentlemen openly recognized that John Moyo was a 'distinguished' man in his own right.

The seventh miracle, which indeed was a miracle of miracles, was that the white visitors without one exception shook hands with a black man for the first time in their lives. John Moyo and Samuel Shava could not but feel that a real change had taken place in these white men.

The eighth miracle was that they drank tea together! Except of course for Tom Dawson, none of them had ever done that before. Some of them had broken their cups if a black man had by mistake used them.

These miracles could only take place in Rhodesia or South Africa, and nowhere else, which is a sad commentary! In any normal society these things could not have been regarded as miracles or progress. It is only in a sick society that an ordinary gathering of men, or parking a car in front of a house, or being ushered in through the front door, or listening to a member of a different race, or exchanging ideas and views, or to address another man properly and affectionately, or ordinary handshaking, or drinking tea together, is considered a miracle. If Rhodesian society had been normal no miracles could have taken place that evening.

'Good night—and congratulations to you both,' said Tom Dawson.

'Good night,' answered the two Sons of the Soil, and the blue Volkswagen zoomed away from the miracle scene.

3

Guilty of Love

'Silence in court!'

Everyone suddenly stopped talking, looked up in expectation, their eyes fixed on the side door from which the voice had emerged. You could hear a pin drop.

Then in came a white magistrate, and everyone rose to their feet. The magistrate gravely moved to his seat. He stood erect before the people, almost sixty of them—men and women, black and white. He bowed stiffly, and the people bowed in acknowledgement. He took his seat, and the people took their seats.

In the dock was a 23-year-old African man dressed in a single-breasted blue suit. Advocate Robert Young appeared for the Crown, but the accused, Jeremiah Fambandoga, was not represented. He had decided to conduct his own defence.

Advocate Robert Young outlined the case for the Crown for about five minutes. Then Detective Inspector John Beans gave an account of a white girl who had handed to him a letter written by the accused, and how he subsequently arrested the accused who made to him a voluntary statement and signed it in the presence of three police witnesses.

The accused's letter appeared as Exhibit A. This was passed to His Worship who then read it to himself in silence. Then he passed it to the court orderly who placed it on a table. The accused's signed and witnessed statement appeared as Exhibit B.

'Have you any questions to put to the inspector?'

'No, Your Worship,' replied the accused.

Detective Inspector Beans then left the witness box.

Miss Jane White, the complainant, was then sworn.

'Do you know the accused?' asked the prosecutor.

'Yes.'

'Can you tell this court what happened between you and the accused?'

Jane White told the court that the accused had made advances to her on three different occasions by word of mouth and that on each occasion she had clearly told him that he should never do a thing like that to a white girl. It was against the law to do such a thing. But the accused had paid no heed. Then she gave an account of an objectionable letter she had received from the accused. She had had no alternative but to take the letter to the police.

'Have you any questions to put to Miss White?' asked the magistrate.

'Yes, Your Worship,' answered the accused.

Jeremiah Fambandoga rose to his feet. 'In your statement to this court you referred to an objectionable letter? Correct?'

'Yes.'

'What was objectionable in that letter?'

'The whole letter.'

'What was the purpose of that letter?'

'To ... well, to make advances to me.'

'And are you saying that it is objectionable for a young man to make advances to a girl?'

The complainant was silent.

'Or put it this way: are you saying it is objectionable for a girl to have advances made to her?'

'It's never done, you see!'

At this juncture the members of the public who had come to hear the case burst into subdued laughter, but quickly cut it off.

'How old are you, Miss White?'

'Twenty.'

'Have you never had advances made to you by anyone else besides me?'

'Yes.'

'In other words, it *is* done?'

'But only . . . only . . . between a white girl and a white man.'

'Suppose the letter I wrote to you had been written by a white man of my age, would you have regarded it as objectionable, assuming, of course, that the contents were the same?'

'No, of course not.'

'What makes my letter objectionable to you is that it has been written by a black man rather than by a white man. Correct?'

The complainant was silent.

'You said, Miss White, in your statement to this court that I made advances to you by word of mouth on three different occasions.'

'Yes.'

'Would you tell this court that on one of these occasions I touched your person against your will?'

'No. You didn't.'

'Did you report these three occasions to the police?'

'Yes, I did.'

'What did they say?'

'They said there was nothing they could do since there was no tangible evidence.'

'Was that the reason, then, why you advised me to write you a letter?'

Miss White went pale. The magistrate was visibly uneasy. The prosecutor just gaped at her. Detective Inspector Beans tightened his thin lips in obvious embarrassment. The blacks lit up with subdued excitement. But for fear of being charged with contempt of court they would have cheered Jeremiah Fambandoga: 'Son of the Soil! Son of the Soil!' Court procedure forbade unruly behaviour of this kind. The blacks felt at this juncture that Miss White and the police had trapped the Son of the Soil. They felt that Miss White had encouraged him. 'Poor Son of the Soil, trapped in love!' they whispered in sympathy with him.

'When I was making advances to you, did you feel, Miss White, that I was pestering you?'

'Yes, I did.'

'Did you report this to the police?'

'Yes, I did.'

'Did they sympathize with you in your plight?'

'Yes.'

'Your Worship, I would like Detective Inspector Beans in the witness box. I am through with Miss White.'

Detective Inspector Beans entered the witness box. He looked wary.

'Inspector Beans, did Miss White tell you that I made advances to her three times by word of mouth?'

'Yes.'

'Did she come and tell you each time?'

'No. She only told me afterwards that you had approached her three times.'

'What action did you take then?'

'None. There was no evidence.'

'When did you feel you had evidence?'

'When she gave me your letter to her.'

'But you took no action at all on Miss White's earlier report that I was pestering her?'

'None.'

'I suggest to you that you took no action in spite of a serious report of this nature because you were using Miss White to trap me.'

'Nothing of the sort.'

'I suggest to you that instead of preventing crime, you actually planned it through Miss White.'

'No.'

At that point the court adjourned for tea. People relaxed and began to discuss the morning's proceedings. Jeremiah Fambandoga, the accused, was facing the possibility of a maximum sentence of three years if he was found guilty.

'What justice can he expect in this country?' asked Gideon Namhoinesu.

'None. None,' said George Tongogara.

'The magistrate himself is a believer in white supremacy. And he is expected to administer justice between black and white! Impossible!' cried Gideon Namhoinesu. 'The detective inspector is a disciple of white supremacy. The prosecutor would rather be dead than give up white supremacy. The complainant is an ardent supporter of the same thing. The very law under which the Son of the Soil is being tried stinks with white supremacy. What a mockery of justice!'

'You're right, Son of the Soil,' said George Tongogara. 'Justice between white and white can be done by these courts because they treat one another as equals. So can justice between black and black, because they consider us equals. But justice between black and white, NEVER! Because black and white are treated as unequals.'

'And the worst part of it is that inequality between black and white is actually legalized!' said Namhoinesu.

'Since 1890 not a single white man has been sentenced to death for the murder of a black man, although Africans who murder Africans or Europeans have been. There are also cases of Europeans who murder Europeans being sentenced to death.'

'It's clear of course that no white man can be sentenced to death for murdering a black man. White supremacy forbids it.'

Three knocks on the door were heard. Then 'Silence in court!' followed, and the learned magistrate made his way to his seat, bowed, and sat, and in turn the people bowed and sat. Jeremiah Fambandoga was in the witness box. He was sworn, and he promised to speak the truth, nothing but the truth, and invoked God to help him.

He had entered a plea of not guilty.

'You are Jeremiah Fambandoga?' asked the prosecutor.

'Yes.'

'Of 94, Fourth Street, Harare?'

'Yes.'

'Look at that letter. Do you admit you wrote it?'

'Yes.'

'What was your purpose in writing the letter?'

'To tell Miss White that I loved her.'

'You admit that Miss White told you on three occasions that you should stop that?'

'Yes.'

'You admit that she told you you were pestering her?'

'Yes.'

'Why didn't you stop it when she told you to stop?'

'That's not how it's done.'

'What do you mean?'

'When a girl tells a young man to stop, the young man doesn't just stop like that. He keeps on trying his luck.'

Here the learned magistrate intervened: 'But she had given you her definite no?'

'Yes, Your Worship.'

'And you continued in spite of that?'

'Yes, Your Worship. I think I should explain an important point here. When a girl says "No" there are usually many things involved. She may mean just that, but she may also not mean just that. She may mean something quite different. There are obvious reasons for this. She may wish to test the seriousness of the young man. I kept on making advances to Miss White to prove to her my constancy, which I felt she wanted to see. There was only one way to do this, and that was to keep on without giving up, and when she suggested the idea of a letter I felt this was fair enough. So I poured out my heart on paper without any reservation, to show her that I loved her with all my heart and soul and mind, and I still do in spite of these most embarrassing proceedings.'

A hush fell in the courtroom.

'You see, Your Worship,' continued Jeremiah Famban-doga, 'although Miss White had said "No" in the first place, there was something in her eyes which seemed to be saying, "Don't give up. Keep on trying." '

'Don't you think that was really something in your own mind?' asked the prosecutor.

'That's why I kept on trying, to find out whether it was in my mind or in Miss White's.'

A subdued laugh ran through the courtroom.

'But you know that you are not supposed to do that to a white girl?'

'Well, I see a good number of white men making love to my sisters, and it never occurred to me that I was not supposed to do so to their sisters.'

Whispers of 'The Son of the Soil has spoken well' escaped the lips of the blacks. 'If they fool around with ours, we'll fool around with theirs,' a radical, fire-eating Son of the Soil said to another.

'Do you now see that it was wrong for you to make advances to a white girl?'

'No, I don't. Proposing to a girl can't be wrong.'

'A white girl, that is!'

'A girl, sir. If she hadn't been a girl I would not have made advances to her. It's not the "white" that attracted me, but the girl.'

'You seem to be unaware of the seriousness of the charge you are facing?'

'I can't see how *kunyenga* can be a serious charge.'

'What do you mean by that term?'

'It means in Shona to make love to a girl, and among us, the black people, *kunyenga* can't be a crime at all.'

A flash of sympathy and admiration for the accused registered on the faces of both black and white. Something deeper than mere black and white seemed suddenly to generate a we-feeling.

The time for the addresses came, and the prosecutor was the first to deliver his. He said to a dead silent court:

'Your Worship, the case before the court is that the accused did, in terms of the Immorality and Indecency Act, wrongfully make advances or overtures to the complainant, three times by word of mouth and once by letter.

'The question before the court is: did the accused in fact contravene the said Act?

'First, the accused admits the authorship of the letter. He admits the signature and the contents as being his own. In other words, Your Worship, the accused himself, in spite of entering a plea of "Not Guilty", admits that he did make advances or overtures to the complainant. He makes no bones about it.

'Second, the accused did not challenge the allegation that he made propositions three times by word of mouth before doing so by letter. He has clearly stated before this court that in fact he did make propositions to the complainant.

'Third, in a written, signed, witnessed statement before the police, which statement is presented to this court as Exhibit B, and which he did not challenge, he admits that he did in fact make propositions to the complainant by word and by mouth.

'Fourth, when the Crown put a question to the accused, he replied that he saw nothing wrong with making propositions to the complainant.

'In other words, Your Worship, the testimony of the accused and the testimony of the complainant establish beyond any reasonable doubt that the accused did in fact make advances or overtures to the complainant, thus contravening the Immorality and Indecency Act. The law of the land has been broken. Your Worship, therefore, must find the accused guilty, bearing in mind that if this is not done, the womenfolk will not have the necessary protection. Finding the accused guilty will be in keeping with the spirit of the Act, namely, to protect the womenfolk, and this is absolutely necessary in the interest of law and order.

'The Act provides a maximum penalty of three years imprisonment with hard labour. I pray this court, Your Worship, to impose upon the accused a severe sentence that will act as a deterrent to others of his kind. If the sentence is lenient, crime of this nature will tend to increase rather than decrease.'

'So the womenfolk must be protected from love!' wondered one Son of the Soil to himself. 'It's a sick society.'

'White womenfolk, you see!' muttered another Son of the Soil.

'That's European civilization!' said yet another.

The accused then addressed the court:

'Your Worship, I want to make it clear to this court that deep down my heart, I do not feel guilty, and I still do not plead guilty.

'I am a black man. I react like a black man. I am a natural man. I react like a natural man. According to our culture a man is fully entitled to *nyenga* a woman. According to nature a man is fully entitled to attend to the attractions of a woman. I did not *nyenga* a married but an unmarried woman. Surely, this cannot be regarded as criminal. According to our custom making advances to a girl is not, and cannot be, a crime.

'Your Worship, this court should also remember that white men also propose to black women. . . .'

'That would appear to have nothing to do with this court,' intervened the learned magistrate.

'It has, Your Worship. In case this court finds me guilty, it should exercise leniency because I did what the whites also do.'

The learned magistrate remained glum.

'I also wish to remind this court that it is a natural and cultural right of man and woman to *nyenga* one another. It cannot therefore be criminal.

'I pray this court not to find me guilty because if it did. . . .'

At this point everyone unconsciously leaned forward.

'It will in effect find me guilty of love.'

'Guilty of love,' some voices whispered.

'That's correct. That's what all this farce would amount to,' said one white man quietly.

'The young man is dead right. Guilty of love! What a society!' muttered another sympathetic white man.

'For, indeed, I've not committed any crime. If I had not loved that girl, the question of an alleged crime would never arise. Love in this country has become a crime. If I had proposed to an animal, Your Worship, the alleged crime would be understandable, but not when I have proposed to another human being like myself! I proposed to a girl, a girl, Your Worship. If I am found guilty, then I shall be a victim of a very sick society. If love's reward in this country is imprisonment, then, Your Worship, what is to be the reward of hate?

'Moreover, Your Worship, this thing called love is not man-made. It is God-given. I cannot even explain it to myself although it is right inside me. I don't cause myself to love her. I am caused by something completely outside my control. I just find myself loving her. Why? Only God knows.'

The learned magistrate then announced, 'Judgment will be given this afternoon at three.'

'The case before this court,' began the learned magistrate, 'is whether or not the accused did in fact contravene the Act. The court is not here to make law, but to administer law.

'On his own admission, the accused did in fact pay his addresses to the complainant, first, by word of mouth, and second, by letter. This admission of the accused is corroborated by the evidence of the complainant, and also by Exhibits A and B. Thus, the accused did in fact contravene section 4 of the Act.

'This court has therefore no alternative in the light of these established facts, and in terms of the Act, but to find the accused guilty.

'Have you anything else to say before I pass sentence?'

'Yes, Your Worship. I pray this court to bear in mind that I am still young. I am twenty-three. This is my first conviction. I did not commit the crime of real crime. I did not attempt to rape the accused, nor did I suggest to her to go to bed with me, but I only asked her to reciprocate the deep love I have for her, a strong, deep, divine emotion that binds soul to soul, which is given to us at birth, and which leaves us at death.'

Great silence fell upon the courtroom.

'I sentence you to two years imprisonment with hard labour, but one year is suspended for three years on condition that you do not commit a similar crime within the same period.'

'Silence in court!'

The learned magistrate made his exit.

Jeremiah Fambandoga, the prisoner of love, was duly rushed to the Central Prison, there to remain a prisoner of the state for the next twelve months.

Miss Jane White wept and sobbed, but no one knew why. Only time would tell why.

The trial of Jeremiah Fambandoga had aroused a great deal of interest among the blacks as well as among the whites. The faithful journalists had recorded the trial, and the local press had generously carried it the following morning. It was the talk of the day.

In Salisbury the Sons and Daughters of the Soil made their endless observations.

'You see, the laws of this country are made to inspire fear in the African.'

'Indeed, the European relies heavily on fear to rule us!'

'The Son of the Soil was supposed to fear that white girl, and never dare to *nyenga* her.'

'His only crime is that he did not have the expected fear, and the lesson had to be driven home to him. Hence the severity of the sentence.'

'There's no doubt that the sentence was calculated to inspire fear in African males so that they may never think of a white woman as a woman.'

'But it won't work. Since when have young men been afraid of girls? They just love them!'

'It can't. Sweetest is the most forbidden fruit, as the saying goes.'

The speakers, Abel Chamunorwa and George Zindoga, were in their early 20s, and they were surprised by the attitude of a Zezuru man in his 70s who had worked as a waiter and cook for the white man during the time of the Chartered Company.

'You see, Sons of the Soil,' began Samson Mano. 'Things have changed for good since the white man came to this country.'

'What do you mean?' they both demanded in some disapproval.

'I mean this, Sons of the Soil. During the days of the Chatakomboni, if a black man did what the Son of the Soil did, they either shot him dead or sent him to prison for many years, not a mere two years with one year suspended.'

'I see,' said George Zindoga.

'If a black man during those days ate the deadly honey, they executed him without hesitation. Nowadays they don't do that. Do they?'

'No,' the two young men admitted.

'I was lucky myself,' Samson Mano said, with a twinkle in his eye. 'I should have been executed, you see!'

'Why?'

'Because I ate a lot of deadly honey.'

'Were you not afraid to do that?'

'I was terribly afraid. I ate it trembling.'

'Why didn't you leave it alone then?'

'It was offered to me, you see!'

'Well, you could have turned down the offer, couldn't you?'

'No! Impossible!'

'Why?'

'Because if you turned it down, she would just scream, "Rape!" And sure enough, you hanged for rape.'

'Oh!' they cried.

'It's true, you know!'

'And so?'

'To turn down the offer of the deadly honey incurred death. To accept the offer, while also having the possibility of death if found out, was more practical for survival. I had to eat the deadly honey to survive. If I had refused, I would have reduced my chances of survival. Now, they don't hang the black man for rape these days, do they?'

'No, they don't.'

'You see! Things have changed for the better, Sons of the Soil.'

'They have changed for you, but not for us,' said the two young men.

'Why not?'

'We don't measure progress by the deadly honey!'

The two young men and the septuagenarian Samson Mano could not see eye to eye. Samson Mano had been born early in the century and had lived most of his life during the heyday of white supremacy when the white man was taken for a human god. But the two young men had been born in 1950 and had lived in the 1960s when white supremacy had shrunk from most parts of Africa back to Europe, and when the white man was being taken for an ordinary mortal, as the case of Jeremiah Fambandoga had clearly demonstrated.

'But why don't you measure progress by that?' asked Samson Mano, rather surprised.

'All human beings are expected to do that by nature. There's no particular virtue in eating any honey! It's a natural thing to do.'

'I follow you, Sons of the Soil. Our eyes are different. Our ears are different. We see differently. We hear differently.'

'You see, Son of the Soil,' George Zindoga tried to explain, 'the white man makes deadly what is naturally not deadly. Then he removes the deadly from it, and leaves it in its former natural state, and he calls this progress. And you believe him!'

'Now I see, Sons of the Soil. There's no change towards progress.'

'None at all.'

But not all the Sons of the Soil took this sympathetic line. The black apostles of hate were mischievously jubilant, since the conviction and imprisonment of Jeremiah Fambandoga, according to them, justified their gospel of hate.

'If the Son of the Soil had hated all the white people,' began one of them, 'he would never have fallen in love with that white woman, and he would never have been in this mess.'

'That's right,' said the second apostle.

'You don't love where you hate,' the first apostle tried to emphasize his point.

'Not at all,' agreed the other.

'You see these black idealists. They preach love among all men, but when their converts start loving, they are sent behind iron bars to learn their lesson.'

'You're right. They don't seem to appreciate the fundamental truth that the white man's philosophy of white supremacy is one of hate, and you can't fight hate with love.'

'Quite so. You see the Son of the Soil tried to fight it with love, and what happened to him? He's behind iron bars! And he'll be there for twelve months! Let's hope he'll now learn better to hate the white man.'

'An experience like that should convince him how right we are. The white man must be hated perfectly until he ceases to hate us.'

'Sooner or later, black and white will get tired of their mutual hate, and then the white man will act more sensibly towards the blacks.'

'We can't gain by love, but we've everything to gain by hate.'

But the reaction to Jeremiah Fambandoga's trial, conviction, and sentence did not confine itself to Salisbury only. The various tribes were keenly interested in it.

The Wamanyika tribes occupying most of Manicaland were, as usual, very outspoken on the matter.

'It's difficult to see what the white man is up to,' began Buwejena meditatively. 'Proposing to a girl is an old custom. We call it *kupfimba*.'

'That's it,' agreed Sawanhu.

'If the Son of the Soil had *pfimba*-ed a man, then certainly he deserved to be jailed even for a much longer period. But when he had *pfimba*-ed a girl! Ah ... these people ... these people....'

'They turn holy things into crime,' said Sawanhu.

'*Kupfimba* is an old, old, old custom accepted by our fathers' fathers, and their fathers' fathers too, and accepted by us, their children, and yet the white man today chooses to send us to jail for it,' said Buwejena, shaking his head.

Beyond Manicaland lies Gazaland, occupied mostly by the Ndaus or Shanganas. They also have the same custom and they call it *kugangisa*. The imprisonment of the Son of the Soil shocked and disgusted them.

'If *kugangisa* has become criminal, that's the end of the Ndau people,' observed Johnson Dlakama.

'Indeed,' said Amos Makuyana.

'You *gangisa* first before you can take a girl to wife,' went on Johnson Dlakama.

'I suppose they want us to be like cattle which do not *gangisa*,' said Amos Makuyana. 'They just mate. We can't do that.'

The Southern Province of Rhodesia is occupied mainly by the Vakaranga, the descendants of Monomotapa and Mambo. They are a people with a highly developed sense of fair play. The custom for which the Son of the Soil was serving time was known to the Vakaranga during the days of Monomotapa in the ninth or tenth century A.D., when they first settled in Rhodesia. It continued during the days of Mambo in the seventeenth century up to the present. The Vakaranga call it *kutswetswa* or *kuruma*. It is a time-honoured institution.

'What's wrong with *kuruma* a girl?' asked Tinago.

'I suppose what's wrong in this case is that the Son of the Soil *ruma*-ed a white girl,' replied Zivanai.

'*Kuruma* as a custom has nothing to do with whiteness. It has something to do with masculinity and femininity,' pointed out Tinago. 'If you impose whiteness or blackness upon it, then you become grossly unfair to the male or female involved.'

'Quite,' softly spoke Zivanai.

Matebeleland is in the west of Rhodesia. Here live most of

the Ndebeles to be found in the country. They too call this custom *ukukhombisa*. To go girl-hunting they call poetically *ukupuma uganga*. Among them, as among other tribes of Rhodesia and beyond, *ukukhombisa* is a healthy, moral, and social thing. Jeremiah Fambandoga's imprisonment on account of *ukukhombisa* was to them a gross injustice bordering on senselessness.

'Until a girl is taken to wife, she remains a legitimate target of romantic arrows,' pointed out one Joseph Thebe.

'Quite so,' agreed Josaka Ndebele. 'And girls like it!'

'Apparently this one didn't.'

'No girl likes all the arrows shot at her.'

'No, of course not.'

'It's her right to send some of them back to the senders.'

'But not to prison.'

'No, certainly not.'

'As a matter of fact, if a girl is not proposed to, we usually feel there's something wrong with her. We get her treated by a *nyanga* so that she becomes a little more arrowable.'

'Right.'

'The same thing is true of a young man who doesn't *khombisa*. We get him treated by a *nyanga* so that he shoots a few more romantic arrows at girls.'

'That's right.'

'It's a strange world we live in when a right thing like that is treated as wrong, and a healthy young man like that has to be shut in prison.'

Other tribes also condemned the whole trial. And among the blacks in Salisbury, especially taxi drivers, bus drivers, truck drivers, clerks, soldiers, policemen, prison warders, cooks, and waiters, there was also a great deal of interest. Almost to a man they praised the Son of the Soil behind the iron bars because he had proposed to a white girl, not because they fancied a white girl was different from a black one but because she was not supposed to be proposed to by a black man! The Son of the Soil suddenly became their hero. They repeated again and again his words in court that he still loved the white girl! He had said that right in front of a white magistrate, a white prosecutor, a white detective inspector, and before a white and black audience in court! He had not tried to conceal his love for the white girl, and he went beyond that! He told that court that it was his right to *nyenga* a white girl! These admirers of the Son of the Soil vowed that they would take turns to visit him in prison.

But the Daughters of the Soil were perturbed by the romantic behaviour of the Son of the Soil now behind the iron bars. Why did he have to propose to a white girl when they themselves were there? A black young man going for a white girl when there were plenty black girls around! They felt insulted. They were shaken at the very foundation of their girlhood. Some of them looked at themselves in their mirrors to see why they didn't qualify for his attention! Apparently, they had forgotten in a moment of injured female pride that love has always been colour-blind.

But interest in the trial of the Son of the Soil was not confined only to the blacks; it spread among the whites as well. It travelled like a wild fire and covered the whole country in no time. To most whites, their world seemed to be fast coming to an end. How dare a black man write such an amorous letter to a *white* girl? Was there something wrong with his eyes? Didn't or couldn't he see that the girl was *white*? Was this the only black man who had done that, or were there other black men of his kind? Their fearful imaginations multiplied the number out of all proportion, and as each multiplicand produced a bigger product, their world collapsed about their ears. How dare a black man tell a white magistrate that he still loved the *white* girl? How dare a black man say that he saw nothing wrong with proposing to a *white* girl? Had the white man become that cheap in the eyes of the black man? Had the black man ceased to fear the white man so that he dared to address his romantic feelings to a *white* girl instead of to a black girl? Darkness seemed to descend. A topsy-turvy world! A black man proposing to a *white* girl! Little did it occur to their minds that the Sons of the Soil had also the same problem. A topsy-turvy world! A Son of the Soil jailed for proposing to a girl!

'Something has got to be done!' roared John Cooper.

'And soon too!' bellowed Robert Lewis.

'The government is getting lax,' said Cooper.

'They must tighten up everything,' said Lewis.

'The Act should provide a higher sentence than a mere three years for a thing like *that*.'

'Three years is too little, I agree.'

'Ten to fifteen years would be more realistic.'

'He's got only two years! How ridiculous the law can be!'

'And of that one year is suspended so that the skelm will serve only one year! Ridiculous!'

'The black man must be taught to leave the things of the white man severely alone. It must be hammered into his thick skull!'

John Cooper and Robert Lewis did not remember that it was the white man who first interfered with the things of the black man. Little did the two white gentlemen pause to consider that the Coloured population of Rhodesia was in fact due, in large measure, to the fact that the white man had interfered with the things of the black man. Little did the two white gentlemen realize that the many Coloured children who had been disowned by their white fathers for social reasons and for reasons of white supremacy, and through no fault of their own, were the direct result of the fact that the white man had interfered with the things of the black man. Little did the two white gentlemen realize that a sizeable number of white men throughout the country bedded night after night with black women, and thus interfered with the things of the black man. If the white man had left alone the things of the black man, probably the black man would have also left alone the things of the white man!

In any case, the argument is all wrong. Women are not things. They are persons and because they are persons, they are not the things of the white man or the black man. The emphasis on white as though this transcends the person of a person causes many white people to distort the humanity of the black man.

'It all started with these missionaries,' observed Lewis. 'Now the black man with a veneer of Western education thinks he's the white man's equal. Oh, how I long for those Charter days when we just shot them dead for doing a thing like that!'

'And there's this clever witchdoctor of theirs befriended by all the white missionaries,' said Cooper. 'They encourage him to believe that he's an equal of the white man!'

'The missionary should never have taught the black man the things of the white man. Jesus should have been enough for the black man.'

'It's high time these missionaries were sent back to where they came from. They have spoilt the black man.'

'In future, I wish no black man would be tried in court for a thing like that. He should be shot dead, and that will teach him the lesson.'

'I agree. Trying a black man in court gives him unnecessary prestige.'

But there were a few whites who did not see Jeremiah Fambandoga's case in quite the same way. Mr and Mrs Jason Swift were among these.

'Just imagine, Mary,' said Jason Swift to his wife, 'if I were a black man, and your parents had me for their son-in-law! Terrible! Wouldn't it be?'

'Terrible for whom, my dear?' asked Mary without looking at her husband.

'For them of course!'

'I don't know about that, my dear.'

'What do you mean?'

'Well, you see, Jason, I don't think a woman marries so that her parents may have a son-in-law. A woman marries first and foremost for her own sake.'

'How about men in that case?'

'You should know that better.'

They looked at each other and smiled with understanding.

'But, Mary, can you imagine going to bed with a black man?'

'I really don't care for a black man, any more than for any other white man than you. No man loves a woman because she's white. No man loves a woman because she's black. No man loves every woman unless he's abnormal or something. He loves her because she's *that* woman. By the same token, no woman loves a man because he's white. No woman loves a man because he's black. No woman loves every man, unless . . . you know. She loves him because he's *that* man.'

'You can't blame the black man,' said Jason Swift. 'It's the white man who passes the law, and it's the white man who breaks it again. After all, the blacks are men and they get hurt when the white man goes out with their women; but the white man forbids them to go out with theirs. It's not fair, is it?'

'Indeed it isn't.'

'The law as it stands is so unrealistic. It cuts across human nature. See what happens in South Africa. A white man falls in love with a black woman he wants to marry; he must leave South Africa and go and live elsewhere with his black wife. Similarly, black men also leave South Africa with their white girls, whom they can marry outside South African borders.'

'Go on, my dear.'

'Take the present case, for instance. Do you think any decent and right-thinking African would continue to have faith in the justice of the white man in this country? It is the white man himself who, by unrealistic and unfair laws, undermines that faith, and we badly need it. The world is no longer as white as it used to be thirty years ago. We have no alternative but to do to the black man what we would he should do to us. That is the only formula of peace and co-operation.'

The reactions to Jeremiah Fambandoga's case gave expression to deep-seated suspicions and fears, but one thing was clear above everything else. The whites heavily underscored *white* while the blacks underlined *girl*, and hence the conflict. The blacks, in the interest of the universal custom of *kunyenga*, stressed the fact of *girl*, but the whites, in the interest of white supremacy, emphasized the fact of *white*. Who should decide the issue? The justice of the white man tended, in this case, to be more concerned with accidental superficialities than with human realities. They felt that white supremacy was for the white man more important than justice, whereas for the black man justice was more important than white supremacy.

Little had the learned magistrate realized that in putting the black man on trial for the things of his heart, he was also putting the white man's justice on a severer trial. The white man's justice was unanimously found guilty of injustice!

'Good morning to you, Jane,' said the Reverend Neil Grant with a welcoming smile.

'Good morning, Father,' answered Jane.

'You haven't been around here for a long time,' said the priest, showing her to a chair. 'I thought you were working in Bulawayo.'

'I was, Father. But I very much wanted to come to Salisbury. You see, my fiancé left prison only a month ago, and he's got a job here in Salisbury, and so I decided to come here so that we can see more of each other.'

'I see. That's interesting.'

'I waited for him all the time he was in prison.'

'Not many girls would do that. How long did you have to wait for him?'

'Exactly eight months.'

'Eight months is a long time to wait.'

'Yes.'

'Did you visit him in prison?'

'Yes, Father.'

'How often?'

'Every month end.'

'That was good of you, Jane. It's good you truly love him, and the knowledge that he had your love must have given him a lot of strength. He had someone to look forward to.'

'I've never loved a man so much in all my life, and this is why I've come to see you, Father. You see, we want to marry.'

'Good, Jane. Marriage is a holy thing. It is ordained of God. The human race depends upon this institution. How old are you, Jane?'

'I'm now twenty-one.'

'And your fiancé?'

'Twenty-four.'

'That's a good age-difference between you. When do you intend getting married?'

'Oh, next month.'

'What's the lucky young man's name?'

'Jeremiah.'

'I see. Where does he work?'

'Here in Salisbury.'

'Where exactly?'

'At Life Insurance Building.'

'As what?'

'As a clerk.'

'Fine. What's his surname?'

'Fambandoga.'

'Fambandoga! That's African, isn't it?' asked the priest in some apprehension and concern.

'Yes, Father.'

For a while the man of God was completely at a loss. He did not know how to react although he tried hard to conceal his feelings. Power of speech deserted him for a moment. Jane White was actually in love with Jeremiah Fambandoga of all men! How had it happened?

'The name sounds familiar to me,' said the priest recovering slightly. 'Surely Jeremiah Fambandoga was the young man who. . . .'

'Yes, Father, I can explain that.'

She gave an account of how Jeremiah first proposed to her and what she thought of the whole thing then. She had thought Jeremiah had taken her for a white prostitute, and she reported the matter to the police to reciprocate the wound his action had inflicted on her.

'Then what caused the change?' asked the priest.

'In court Jeremiah clearly said he loved me. He said although he was in trouble, he still loved me.'

'And then?'

'When the magistrate found him guilty, he said he was not guilty of any crime but of love. How could a man be guilty of love? How could a man be jailed for love's sake? I vowed in my heart that I was going to demonstrate to him that he was not guilty of love. Love can't be a crime.'

'So what did you do?'

'At the end of the same month he was sent to jail, I went to see him. I apologized to him, and I told him I loved him with all my heart, mind, and soul. He smiled at me and said, "I'm serving time for you, my love." Father, I want you to marry us next month.'

Silence fell upon them. The priest was at a loss. This was the first case of its kind in his parish, which he had served well and faithfully for ten years.

'A little while ago, Jane,' the priest ended the silence, 'you told me that you had been working in Bulawayo?'

'Yes, Father.'

'Do you mean to tell me that at the end of every month you came to Salisbury only to see him?'

'Yes, Father.'

'For how long were you allowed to see him?'

'Fifteen minutes.'

'Only that?'

'Only fifteen minutes. I looked forward to those fifteen minutes every month.'

'I see.'

'Then you'll marry us?'

'Oh, I've not said that.'

'What do you say?'

'I cannot tell you anything now.'

'Why can't you, Father?'

'This is a serious thing.'

'Why, Father?'

'Such things are not done.'

'Why not?'

'Well, our custom doesn't allow it.'

'What custom?'

This was a crucial question for the man of God. What custom did the man of God follow? Broadly, there were two sets of custom. There was the custom of the State, and there was also the custom of the Church. Which did the man of God mean? What was the custom of the State? It was white supremacy, and all other customs derived from this one. What was the custom of the Church? It was love, and all other Christian customs stemmed from this one. Was the Christian Church in the service of Christian love or white supremacy? If the man of God refused to marry Jane and Jeremiah, would such an act be motivated by Christian love or by white supremacy? What custom does not allow black and white to marry? The full weight of Jane's question staggered the man of God. He felt he now stood at crossroads.

'As I've already said to you, Jane, this is a serious matter,' said the priest. 'I shall have to report it to our church committee. I shall certainly keep in contact with you.'

'Thank you, Father.'

'And thank you too for opening your heart like this to me.'

Jane left the priest's study, and the priest closed the door behind her. He was sweating. He paced the floor, and next he was on his knees praying. 'God,' he said quietly, 'show us the way, the way that is pleasing in thy sight.'

Speech died on his lips, but he remained on his knees silent in prayer. His eyes were shut, and he was motionless for quite some time. 'Show us the way, oh God,' he again repeated to himself. Silence again wrapped him up, and again he broke it with 'Thy will be done, oh Lord.' He stood up, paced the floor of his study, and stood still and silent. Then he cried out, 'God, show me the way! . . . Thy will, oh God!'

He went to the chair behind his desk and heaped himself there in meditation.

Jane had placed a heavy burden on his soul, and he was now struggling with it. Two voices seemed to speak to him. Which one was he to obey? He had been a priest for ten years, and his parishioners had known him as a man who would rather obey God than men. God had commanded: 'Love ye one another,' and the priest had obediently preached many a brilliant sermon on that. But now before him were these two young people. They loved each other to the point of marrying each other. They were a response to God's own command to love one another. But white supremacy commanded to the contrary. Whose servant was he? God's or the White Dragon's?

He was going to lose many of his church members if he approved of the proposed marriage. The church would lose not only in membership, but in finances as well. Most probably he would even lose his own job. He would also be in danger of being lynched or ostracized by some of the whites on whom he depended for his social and cultural intercourse. His children were sure to be ridiculed and jeered at by other white children. The White Dragon told him all this as he stood before him breathing fire and threats.

He reported the case to the church committee, which was duly convened a week after that.

The committee comprised nine elders; the priest was also part of it.

A short prayer was said at the beginning to invoke God's guidance throughout the proceedings, the outcome of which was eagerly awaited, not only by the parishioners but by the European community in general; and the African nationalists, too, were particularly keen about the outcome.

The priest recounted his interview with Jane the previous week and the whole committee listened very carefully.

'How old did you say this girl was, Father?' asked Elder Martin.

'She's twenty-one,' replied the priest.

'Would you say, Father,' continued Elder Martin, 'that she's a normal girl?'

'In my own judgement she is perfectly normal,' replied the priest.

'The question of her normality,' put in Elder Jackson, 'is relevant to the issue before us. If she were not normal, then the next thing we should do would be to get a psychiatrist for her, and forget all about the matter. But since you say you think she is perfectly normal, then we have to deal with the matter. We have no alternative.'

'Before we do that, however,' intervened Elder Martin, 'I must say I find it difficult to accept the normality of a girl who in one breath literally hands a young man to the police, and then in the next breath hands him over to the priest!'

'Well, if I may speak for her in the light of what she told me herself,' said the priest, 'it was during the trial of this young man that the girl felt convinced that he truly loved her. She then repented of her error in handing him over to the police.'

'Have you, Father, checked whether she is regarded as normal by her own associates?' asked Elder Jacobson.

'Yes, I have. I checked with her previous employers in Bulawayo, and they speak of her in glowing terms. The same thing is true of her employers here in Salisbury.'

The committee was satisfied that she was normal, and that the case before them should therefore be looked into as carefully as possible.

'The question that is before this committee is that this girl wants to marry this young man. If the young man had been white, there would have been no difficulty at all. But the difficulty now arises because this young man is black, and this girl is white. This girl wants me to marry them. What does our local church here say?' The priest posed the question.

'Brethren,' spoke up Elder Hadfield, 'as Christians the issue here is quite clear. In Christ Jesus there's neither Jew nor Greek. For our situation this injunction of St Paul's becomes, "In Christ Jesus, there's neither black nor white."'

'While that is scripturally true, Mr Hadfield, it is also equally true that in the State there's such a thing as black and white,' pointed out Elder Henderson. 'This is a fact in law.'

'While that is in fact so, Mr Henderson,' said Elder Hadfield, 'we are not here, I think, to decide for the State. The question before us is not, "What does the State say about marriage between black and white?" We all know that the State says "No!" But the question before us is, "What does our local church say about marriage between black and white?" '

'Frankly, brethren,' chipped in Elder Kennedy, 'I think the time has not yet come that black and white can marry.'

'When do you think the time will come?' asked Elder Henderson.

'When the white people in this country are ready.'

'And when will that be? Remember, Mr Kennedy, that they have been in this country for the last 83 years. When do you think they will be ready?' asked Elder Henderson.

'That's difficult to say,' admitted Elder Kennedy.

'But this girl is ready to marry a black. So the time has come, in fact,' pointed out Elder Henderson.

'I think, myself, the time came as far back as 1900 when the white man began cohabiting with black women,' said Elder Hadfield. 'The only way of preventing black and white living in sin is that they be properly married, and the church must take its stand on this case.'

'Father Grant, you have been rather quiet,' observed Elder Martin. 'What do you say?'

'Well, if these two young people want to marry, there's nothing that can stop them. Love is a thing of the heart. When two souls have found each other, who can separate them? The two have loved each other, and we must accept that as an act of God, and therefore we must not interfere with it. This is true liberty although the State here is against marriages across colour lines. But, for the Church, that is of course neither here nor there. The Church must marry those who desire to be married regardless of what the State says against it.'

'But, Father, remember,' cautioned Elder Kennedy, 'that it is written in the Bible, "Render unto Caesar that which is Caesar's, and to God that which is God's."'

'I remember that, Mr Kennedy,' answered the priest. 'The real question is, "In this particular case, what is it that is Caesar's and what that is God's?" When Jesus said this he was answering a specific question relating to the payment of tax. Was tax to be paid to Caesar or God? Of course to Caesar. Caesar had made the coins and therefore the coins were to be paid to him. But the soul belongs to God, and not to Caesar. In the deep matters of the soul such as love, only God and these young people are involved. The State cannot have sovereignty over the people's souls. The souls of these young people have interlocked, intertwined, and fused, and have become one in two, and that is now an affair between them and God, and the State has no business to interfere.'

'If we allowed the State to interfere,' said Elder Hadfield, 'this would be the worst form of dictatorship—a dictatorship that even dictates to the soul area of man! It's the person who's in love, not the State, and the State has therefore no business to interfere in such matters.'

After a lot of exchange of Christian insights, the committee agreed that they were not opposed to the proposed marriage between the two young people, although this was against the law of the State. The priest was to convey the answer to Jane at his earliest convenience.

'The church has agreed that I marry you and your fiancé,' he told her.

'Oh, wonderful, Father!'

'But it cannot be in this country, as you well know.'

'But where then, Father?'

'Well, in some neighbouring country where there is not this scourge of white racism. Some of my church members have already donated money so that you and your fiancé can leave the country. I'll fly together with the two of you.'

'I can never thank you enough, Father. But isn't it terrible that we have to fly away just to get married?'

'Terrible indeed. My church members in doing all this are merely atoning for the sin the white man has committed in this country. Sometimes I really feel ashamed I am white.'

'Jeremiah will be so excited to hear all this.'

'I'm sure he will. But remember, it means that after you are married you cannot come back and live here as husband and wife because this is against the law. You'll have to wait until the Africans take over before you return to this country to live together. It may be a long wait, or only a short one. It all depends upon how events in this country move.'

'I understand, Father.'

Two months later Jane and Jeremiah and the priest were seen boarding an airliner, and just before they entered the plane a roar of 'Son and Daughter of the Soil!' arose from a wildly cheering crowd of about five hundred Sons and Daughters of the Soil. It was the biggest moment of Jane's life. She felt proud to be affectionately addressed as 'Daughter of the Soil'. She waved back in acknowledgement. The three passengers disappeared into the plane, and the mechanical bird majestically and gracefully took to the clear blue sky and made for the country where the Son and Daughter of the Soil could be married without the threats of the White Dragon.

4

A Conspiracy against Democracy

'This witchdoctor of theirs is going around the country stirring up trouble among the natives,' said Keith Lambert,
placing his glass of beer on a small round mahogany table.

'The sooner we show the black man that the white man
means to rule this country now and in years to come, the
better,' said Peter Benson.

'But as long as this witchdoctor is allowed to go round
addressing these natives, we'll have serious trouble on our
hands,' warned Lambert.

'The police should stop the meetings,' agreed Benson.

Three other white men also sitting at the table just sipped
their beer and listened.

'I gather he's resigned his lectureship at the university so
that he can devote more time to brewing trouble,' said Keith
Lambert.

'How much were they paying him there?' asked Benson.

'Oh, I gather round $300 per month.'

'And he's left all that!' cried Benson.

'Apparently.'

'There you are,' Benson jeered. 'A black man is a black
man. No sense of values. Fancy leaving all that money for a
wild goose chase.'

'You train them and give them European values, and soon
they slip back into theirs!' said Lambert.

'Mark you, he's very serious about black politics,' said
Benson, frowning thoughtfully.

'I dare say,' answered Lambert. 'But we've got to teach this witchdoctor that he's trying the impossible.'

'The white man is here to rule.'

'That's right.'

'And to rule for ever!' Lambert went on, shouting as if trying to make John Moyo hear it wherever he was.

'But,' began one of the silent three, a newcomer to the country, 'if Dr Moyo organizes the blacks, and gets the blacks behind him, that's democratic, and this would be fair, surely.'

'That's just the trouble, Bob,' replied Lambert.

'What trouble?' asked Bob Johnson, puzzled.

'What trouble?' Lambert repeated the question to give himself time to think out the answer. 'Well, democracy, of course.'

'How do you mean?'

'You can't talk of democracy in this country. Never!'

'But I thought our government was democratic!'

'So it is for us, but if you treat the black man democratically, which is the sort of rubbish the witchdoctor is demanding, then the white man is finished politically. He'll cease to be the ruler of this country.'

'I see what you mean. So how do you propose settling the present political deadlock between black and white?'

Silence fell upon the five men. The others all looked at Keith Lambert. He frowned thoughtfully.

'You see, Bob,' he began, 'you must remember the clear lessons of history if you're to appreciate the present problem. These ungrateful natives now want to kick us out of the country which we've done so much to develop. That is what the witchdoctor wants. Black rule means that.'

'You've just said that we should remember the clear lessons of history,' said Bob Johnson. 'What are these?'

'You remember what Bismarck once said? The great issues of the day will not be solved by majority resolution, but by iron and blood.'

'And so?'

R.R.—3*

'The great issues of Rhodesia will not be solved by majority nonsense which that witchdoctor preaches to those innocent natives, but by iron and blood.'

Silence again descended upon them as each man considered these hard words which seemed to prophesy hard times ahead of the whole country.

Lambert went on, 'You remember, also, what Adolf Hitler says in his *Mein Kampf*?'

'No. What does he say?'

'That which diplomacy will not give us the fist will. There's a lesson for the white man in these words,' said Lambert, looking dead earnest. 'If the deadlock between black and white cannot be settled by ordinary diplomacy, then the fist —or let's say the bullet—must give us the settlement we want.'

'What do you expect diplomacy to give you?' asked Johnson.

'Absolute control of this country.'

'How are you going to set about it diplomatically to convince the black man to give you absolute control of this country?'

'Promise him that the white man will rule him fairly.'

'But the black man doesn't want to be ruled fairly by the white man!' protested Johnson. 'He wants to rule himself. You are thinking of the white man ruling the black man, but the black man is thinking of ruling himself. My question then is: how can your diplomacy resolve this deadlock if you are not prepared to use democratic means?'

'Democracy, no. I've said that already.'

'If you rule out democracy, then you have ruled out diplomacy as well.'

'Quite so.'

'Therefore, you see, you cannot justifiably say, that which diplomacy will not give the white man the bullet will. By ruling out democracy, and hence diplomacy, you've left yourself only with one course of action—shooting the black man.'

'In the final analysis, I'm afraid, it means just that,' said Lambert grimly.

'I suppose you're aware that in opting for the bullet, you've actually deserted democracy, which is the very foundation of Western government.'

'In a way you're correct.'

'Are you aware that you're deserting democracy at a time when Communism is making real headway in Africa?'

'Yes, I am aware of it. But the white man in this country has no alternative but to desert democracy.'

'What you really mean is that the white man in this country has no alternative but to strengthen the hand of Communism?'

'Oh, no, I'll have no truck with Communism.'

'But that is the effect of your discarding democracy. You turn the black man into an enemy of the white man here, and since he wants to rule himself, and since the Soviet Union and the People's Republic of China and other Communist countries are open supporters of the black man's cause, you'll have more than you can cope with.'

'I think,' chipped in Malcolm Avery, who had been listening keenly, 'that Bob has pinpointed the problem facing this country. The white man wants, and is determined, to rule the black man. But the black man does not want to be ruled. He wants, and is determined, to rule himself. As a result of these two divergent positions there's a deadlock between black and white in this country. The question now arises: can this deadlock be solved democratically? Lambert maintains it cannot. The next question then is: can this deadlock be solved by the use of guns? Lambert maintains it can. Assuming that we settle for now on the bullet, what would be the effect of this?'

'What do you mean, Malcolm?' asked Bob Johnson.

'What I mean is: can the white man win by using the bullet to resolve this deadlock?'

'I have already stated,' said Lambert, looking very much concerned, 'that democracy is the white man's political grave in this country. On that one I am absolutely convinced.'

'And the bullet?' asked Johnson.

'What about it?' asked Lambert.

'Very difficult to state what I mean. Put it this way. If democracy is the white man's political grave in this country, what political function has the bullet?'

'It will give the white man absolute control of this country,' answered Lambert.

'And you believe that?' asked Johnson.

'Yes, of course,' answered Lambert with an air of self-assurance.

Bob Johnson shook his head with disbelief.

'Do you know how we came to possess this land?' Lambert asked. He disappeared into his house, and then returned with a rifle and a packet of bullets. 'You see,' he said, holding the rifle up. 'This is what helped us to possess this land. This is what has enabled us to rule the natives here for almost a hundred years. And this is what will help us to continue in the possession of this land.'

'Historically you are dead right,' admitted Johnson.

'Democracy had nothing to do with our ruling the natives the last hundred years. Had it?'

'No.'

'Democracy has nothing to do with our ruling the native today. Has it?'

'There's a big question-mark today,' replied Johnson.

Ignoring the remark, Lambert gently tossed the rifle into the air and as it yielded to the force of gravity he caught it in mid-air and proudly said, 'This is what has enabled the white man to hold his own. Not that thing of yours—democracy.'

Bob Johnson made no comment.

'When we came here a hundred years ago,' said Lambert, 'we did not need democracy to possess this beautiful land. To rule for the last hundred years democracy did not have to come into the picture at all. Why democracy today?'

'Because times have changed,' answered Johnson.

'For us, yes. But not for the natives!'

'For them as well.'

'Oh, no, the natives are still exactly as they were a hundred years ago. They still marry by the dozen, breed like rats, follow their many superstitions.'

'Oh, but you're quite wrong, Keith. There are many Christian schools where you find thousands of them learning and this is change.'

'What is Christianity to a native? What does it mean to him? Absolutely nothing. Waste of effort to try to christian-ize these primitives.'

'Well, at any rate Dr Moyo has the blacks behind him. He has more followers than any European leader at present. He's a force to reckon with.'

Lambert laughed cynically and held up his box of bullets.

'You see,' he said, 'the big witchdoctor has numbers, but the white man has bullets. I've no faith in democratic or numerical power, but I have inexhaustible faith in bullet power.'

'You sound very much like Mao Tse-Tung. He says political power is in the barrel of a gun.'

'He's dead right,' enthusiastically commented Lambert.

'You're very Communist in your theory of political power, you see!'

'Not at all. If I say 2 plus 2 is 4 and a Communist says the same, or conversely, if a Communist says 2 plus 2 is 4, and I also give the same answer, I do not automatically qualify as a Communist, do I?'

'But you sound like one. Communists believe in the armed struggle, and you also believe in that. African freedom fighters believe in that too. The white man has no earthly reason whatsoever to condemn either the Communists or the African freedom fighters.'

'We seem to be getting away from the heart of the matter,' Malcolm Avery pointed out. 'This is not an academic question. Suppose we accept for the purposes of argument that we follow the theory of bullet power to resolve the present deadlock between black and white. According to Keith, this would give the white man absolute control of this country in the face of growing Black Power. Is this a valid proposition?'

'Well, Malcolm,' said Lambert, 'there's no such thing as Black Power, at least according to me.'

'Why not?' asked Bob Johnson.

'Because Black Power is numbers, and numbers, in my opinion, are not power in the face of bullet power.'

'I see,' nodded Johnson. 'Now, Keith, suppose we follow your Bismarckian theory of "iron and blood", how far would this carry us? You are no doubt aware that that policy cost three wars instigated by Bismarck, and that these three wars resulted in the loss of 80,000 lives!'

'We've no alternative but to follow the road of iron and blood.'

'And no doubt, you're aware that Hitler's "fist" methods cost about 24 million lives?'

'Your comparison of our situation with that of Bismarckian or Nazi Germany is not valid. There's no comparison between the two situations.'

'There is! You advocate "iron and blood" or the bullet, which is what the German leaders did.'

'But Bismarck and Hitler had expansionist motives. They wanted to grab other people's territory. That is not the reason why I advocate the bullet. We don't intend grabbing other people's territory. That's not our reason for the bullet.'

'What is your reason?'

'To keep what we've got.'

'You mean what we grabbed a hundred years ago?'

'Well, well, as you please.'

Mrs Lambert appeared from the house. 'There's a phone call for you, Mr Johnson,' she called.

Bob Johnson followed her and after three minutes he returned. 'I'm sorry, I have to leave right away. Thanks for the beer, Keith.'

He exited, got into his Mercedes Benz, and roared away.

'Well, I'm glad he's gone,' sighed Peter Benson.

'He's not one of us,' observed the hitherto silent Donald Parker. 'He thinks of democracy as though he were in Britain or France. This is Africa. This is Rhodesia. If the white man is to stay here, then to hell with democracy!'

'Democracy is for the white man in this country, and we intend keeping it so,' said Benson coming out of himself.

'The witchdoctor can have his overwhelming numbers,' ridiculed Lambert. 'But he'll soon learn as others before him have learned. Nehanda learned it the hard way. Kagubi also learned it the hard way. We hanged them for brewing the 1896 rebellion. Mapondera tried the same thing in 1900 and he died in the Salisbury prison serving a seven-year jail sentence. This celebrated witchdoctor will follow his kind. It's a matter of time.'

'All right, we've heard all that stuff,' intervened Malcolm Avery. 'But what concrete steps must the white man take now to ensure his position? This, I believe, is what really faces us.'

'That's true,' agreed Parker. 'One thing that is clear is that all the natives in this country are now under the magic spell of this witchdoctor.'

'In fact, the natives have come to think and speak of him as their messiah,' said Benson. 'They think he's much stronger than the white man.'

'And this is very dangerous,' warned Parker. 'The white man must strip him of his followers before things go too far.'

'Agreed,' nodded Lambert. 'But how?'

'I tell you what,' said Parker, brightening with inspiration. 'We have many of his followers who are employed by the white man. All our industries, commerce, communications, and transport, as well as government service, employ a large number of his followers. Sack the most important of them for the slightest mistake. It will quickly dawn upon their minds that it is too costly for them to follow this witchdoctor. It will affect their jobs, their wives, their children, and their beer, and then they'll desert the witchdoctor.'

'That sounds as though it might work!' said Benson eagerly.

'The police should also get cracking on his followers,' added Keith Lambert. 'Let them harass his supporters, arrest them, keep them in police cells a day or so for interrogation, then release them. This will drive the lesson home.'

'The police could do a lot, you know,' said Avery, 'and the natives are sure to desert him. They're such cowards.'

'But we have a problem here,' added Lambert. 'How about the natives in the African Tribal Trust Lands? He has unbelievable support among these too.'

'Yes, I know,' agreed Benson, 'but the District Commissioner can effectively deal with those. He controls all the boys in the T.T.L.s, and they just tremble before him.'

'That's a very practical step,' commended Avery.

'How about the natives at mission schools or farms?' asked Benson.

'We'll have to move more cautiously with those,' advised Parker. 'American missionaries, as the early history of this country shows, are just impossible. They'll side with the native all the time.'

'I would say this is true of most foreign missionaries, except our British missionaries,' said Avery. 'But even *they* are now getting spoilt like the American ones.'

'But,' chipped in Lambert, 'we must get cracking at the mainstream of his supporters so that they are made to feel the error of their ways. It's important that we impress upon the mind of the government the absolute necessity for more military training—more whites and more of our natives must be called up for military training.'

'Right, right,' concurred Avery.

'The sooner the better,' emphasized Parker. 'The black man must be left in no doubt that the white man here means to be boss of this country.'

'We need more police reservists,' pointed out Benson, looking worried.

'And more army reservists,' added Avery. 'The black man must see with his own eyes that the white man is strong in every way, that he's no match for him. This fact must be hammered into his thick skull.'

'Military parades must be regularly conducted wherever there are large native concentrations so that they can see for themselves that the white man is strong, and therefore that their witchdoctor is leading them astray,' said Parker.

'And, in addition to that, there should be regular military exercises in the various parts of the country,' contributed Avery, 'so that we drive it home to the black man that he's backing a losing horse.'

'I think,' said Lambert, 'restriction will do this witch-doctor some good.'

'Detention would be better,' suggested Parker.

'Once he's detained,' said Avery, 'his many followers will not know what to do. They're just hopeless without him.'

'Prison would be the ideal place for him,' said Benson. 'It would break him down.'

'Oh, but it's difficult to get the skelm convicted,' observed Lambert. 'He's so skilful in his use of English that he picks his way quite easily through the Law and Order (Mainten-ance) Act, which is designed to send such political natives to jail.'

'We'll get him one day,' assured Avery.

'And the blinking natives will desert him the same day,' said Benson.

'But we must never forget,' Lambert reminded them, 'to show the natives and their witchdoctor bullet power in its naked form. Somehow they must be taught the lesson that the white man here opens fire, not to scare, or some silly thing like that, but to kill.'

'Quite right,' affirmed Benson. 'The black man must learn that the white man shoots to kill.'

'There's no other way the white man can survive in this country,' observed Lambert.

'From now on, velvet gloves off,' said Benson. 'Bare fists, and the black man will understand us better.'

The four white gentlemen talked among themselves over

and over, and they were unanimous on one thing, and that was that the white man must slap democracy in the face if he was to survive politically. They were apprehensive of the six million blacks as against themselves who numbered only a quarter of a million. They were determined that the black man was to have no vote, and they reiterated again and again that the vote was the thing of the white man, not the thing of the black man. They suggested ridiculously and unrealistically high voting qualifications which virtually disenfranchised all adult Africans. The idea was to give the African and the outside world an appearance of democracy, while in fact they denied its substance to the African. All this they did to preserve their ideology of white supremacy, which they cared more for than for democracy.

The second point on which they were unanimous was that strong-arm methods were to be used, backed by bullet power. They agreed among themselves that while elsewhere political power was born in the ballot box, in Rhodesia it could not be. It had to be born in the barrel of a gun. They were not concerned with such fundamental questions as: what kind of political power is born in the barrel of a gun? They did not have to ask these questions. They knew the answers already. They knew that democracy was born in a ballot box, and they denied the black man the ballot box so that the black man should not oust them from political power. They knew that white supremacy was born in the barrel of a gun, and they denied the African the gun so that black rule should not be born in the barrel of a gun. The vote generates political power. The bullet generates political power. The four white gentlemen realized this, and they determined that the black man should have neither of these. He must remain politically impotent. As Lambert put it: 'The vote is something for the white man. The bullet is something for the white man. These two, the white man must keep to himself, for his children, and for his children's children.'

It never, however, seemed to occur to these four gentlemen that, if the African was denied the vote through the ordinary democratic processes, then the black man was himself left with no alternative but the bullet to realize democracy in a country that is his by birth. The white man was determined to use the bullet to keep democracy to himself. On the other hand, the black man was equally determined to use the bullet to have democracy extended to himself! Little did the white men realize that while they were piling up bullets to deny the black man democracy, the black man was also piling up bullets to break the white man's monopoly of democracy. The white man was prepared to use violence to deprive the black man of democracy, and the black man was equally prepared to use the same means to make his point. This was the real danger facing the country, and the blame for it could only be laid at the feet of white supremacy.

The third point on which the four gentlemen were agreed was that pressure must be brought to bear upon the white government to tighten up the laws of the country to ensure the survival of the white man. Local M.P.s were to be approached to this end. The social, economic, and political gap between black and white had to be increased so that the black man would at no time come to feel that he was the equal of the white man. Positive measures were to be taken to cause him to feel that he was the natural inferior of the white man, not only in this world, but also in the world to come. In other words, the policy these four gentlemen were advocating was one of fear. They felt the black man had to be made to fear the white man, to give way to him. In short, they were trying to bring back the days of the 1900s when the shooting down of a black man was something of good sport! They advocated arbitrary arrests, detentions, imprisonment, police brutality, as necessary measures to keep the black man in a state of fear, and hence easily manageable by white supremacy, which the black man's newly found self-assertion was threatening from all directions.

'I feel happy,' said Lambert, 'after this practical exercise.'

'It has been a very useful evening,' agreed Avery.

5

A Plot against Dictatorship

'I am disappointed,' said Silas Mushonga. 'The Son of the Soil is talking rather than fighting.'

'The white man is only too pleased to see him going round like that, and not going to the heart of the matter,' agreed Simon Mugadza.

'And yet the Son of the Soil is such an intelligent man! He has real brains!' moaned Silas.

'He's too full of the book. That's his trouble,' asserted Simon Mugadza. 'Books and revolution don't mix. Books are all right after the revolution, but not before.'

'The book has been talking for the last hundred years, and it has got us nowhere. It's about time we allowed a revolution to talk to the white man,' said Silas Mushonga. 'His own democracy can't talk to him. His own Christianity can't talk to him. His own civilization can't talk to him. Only a revolution will talk to him, and he'll listen to it with both ears. But it has to be a well-organized, effective revolution. He's deaf to the rights of the black man, and only a real revolution will cure him of his deafness.'

'This is where the Son of the Soil is entirely wrong,' said Simon Mugadza. 'He seems to believe that by sheer force of eloquence he can change the heart of the white man. He might as well orate to a stone in the hope that it will hear him. Only a revolution will change the heart of the white man. Democracy has failed. Christianity has failed. Sound common-sense has totally failed. Only a real revolution—a bloody one—can change the stone heart of the white man.'

At this point Silas Mushonga and Simon Mugadza were joined by two other Sons of the Soil who were equally disillusioned by John Moyo's political performance. The two arrivals were John Sibanda and Gideon Masuku. The four men were in a small room illuminated by three candles. They represented the down-to-earth Sons of the Soil who believed in Action Now, and talk afterwards.

Silas Mushonga had passed Form 4; he was 26 years old, married, and his wife was expecting a baby. He was a bus driver, and was receiving $60 a month for his job, for which a white driver was paid $160 a month. He had an economic grouse against such a set-up which discriminated against him purely on racial grounds. But he had grasped the central fact that unless and until white supremacy was killed and buried in Rhodesia, and majority rule became the order of the day, he would continue to suffer economic injustice at the hands of the white man.

Simon Mugadza was 35, married, with four children, two girls and two boys. He was a Form 6 fellow and was a salesman in the employment of a white firm which paid him $75 a month, whereas a white man who held the same qualifications and did the same job was paid $200 for the same period. One day he was heard to complain, 'Because I am black, the firm feels it's right that they steal $125 from me every month! Every year they steal from me $1,500! In ten years time they will have stolen $15,000! The rich get richer, and the poor poorer!' It was clear to him that the political set-up was responsible for all this, and he was therefore determined to work for a new political set-up.

John Sibanda was 40 years old. He had been in the prison service for the last ten years. He held a Form 2 educational qualification. He was particularly pained by the fact that he received, after all these years of faithful service, only $50 a month whereas new European prison recruits started at $150 a month! He used to bemoan thus his poor lot: 'It pays to be white, but it doesn't pay to be black!' But more clear-minded Sons of the Soil used to correct him quickly:

'It pays to have majority rule, but it doesn't pay to have minority rule!' And this had sunk into his mind. John Sibanda, a father of six children, found it difficult to make ends meet, and he blamed this on minority rule.

Gideon Masuku was 32, married, with three children. He was Form 6. He was an accountant and earned $80 a month. If the same job had been held by a white man, he would have been paid $300 a month. He was pained by the fact that pay was not according to merit, but according to the colour of a man's skin. The blacker the lower the pay. The whiter the higher the pay. So he believed. White rule must go so that people can be paid according to their merits and not according to the pigment of their skin. Black rule is for the black man, white rule is against the black man. So he thought. He was an ardent supporter of majority rule, and an uncompromising enemy of white supremacy which held him down financially in spite of his efficiency.

'The Son of the Soil has not quite got the mind of the white man,' said John Sibanda. 'He seems to be under the disastrous illusion that he can convince the white man by talking to him.'

'We've been complaining of the same thing,' said Silas Mushonga.

'That's the weakness with all these graduates,' observed Gideon Masuku. 'They seem to think that if they can talk the white man's language correctly, quote him extensively, and behave like the white man they will get somewhere with him. The white liberals literally lead our intellectuals by their noses. They seem to believe anything that these white liberals tell them.'

'Dead right, dead right,' said John Sibanda. 'We must not speak from the position of the white man, but from the position of the black man.'

'Correction, Son of the Soil,' intervened Silas Mushonga. '*Speak* is a wrong word. *Act* is the word.'

'Hear, hear,' they all applauded him. 'Act! Act!'

'The white man has a burning desire to hold the black

man in subservience,' said Gideon Masuku. 'He desires to hold him in social subservience. He desires to hold him in political subservience. In economic subservience. In educational subservience and in national subservience. His white supremacy soul moves him to deny the black man equal opportunity, equal human status, equal fundamental human rights and freedoms. In other words, Sons of the Soil, the white man has a negative soul when it comes to the rights of the black man.'

'Quite so,' cried the other three.

'The black man must act from the position of the black man, and not from that of a white man. He has no soul when it comes to the black man. Make no mistake about that.'

'Only intellectuals would make such a mistake,' said Silas Mushonga.

For a while silence reigned in the candle-lit room. The four Sons of the Soil stared at each other in silence. An on-looker would have returned the verdict: 'No communication between themselves.' But of course this would have been wrong. Although the four men were silent, they were communicating with one another in that silence. Their souls were in communion with one another. They were silently listening to themselves and to one another. They were silently talking to one another. It was communication in silence, and silence in communication! They listened intently to the deep flow of human experience inside them. They heard the groans of the black man under the heavy yoke of white supremacy. They saw the naked determination of the white man to keep it on indefinitely. They saw their own children wearing the same yoke. They saw them growing up with it fastened around their necks until it became accepted as a normal thing to have around one's neck! They saw it as a badge of humiliation distinguishing them from other black men elsewhere in Africa who had thrown it off their necks. They felt humiliated. They felt the heavy yoke of white supremacy was still hanging securely around their proud necks to announce to the whole of Africa and the rest of the world that the black

man in Rhodesia was incapable of inflicting defeat on white
supremacy, which other black men elsewhere in Africa had
so successfully done. All these things, the four Sons of the
Soil felt in silence, suffered in silence, and communicated to
one another in silence.

'You know,' Simon Mugadza broke the silence, 'the white
man in this country lives under illusions. He still believes
that he can hold his own in this country just as he did in 1893
and 1896–7. It does not occur to him that he held his own
then only because we had no guns.'

'Apparently he chooses to ignore that,' said John Sibanda.

'Now the white man has not the monopoly of guns,' said
Silas Mushonga. 'The black man has access to them. The
story will be different.'

'Quite so,' they all answered.

'The white man denies the black man democracy because
he has guns,' asserted Silas Mushonga. 'We must have guns
to destroy the white man's dictatorship in this country. Is
there any earthly reason why we don't have adult franchise
in this country?'

'None! None!'

'It is because they have the guns, and we don't. Guns in
the hands of the white man are equal to dictatorship for the
black man.'

'Right! Right!'

'But we want democracy, and therefore we want guns!'

'And we want them NOW!'

'That's what the Son of the Soil should be telling the
people.'

'Indeed! Indeed!'

'No guns, no majority rule.'

'Dead right!'

'We need guns to smash down the white man's dictatorship.'

'Yes, yes.'

'So that we can establish a democratic state.'

'That's the heart of the matter.'

'The Western countries won't give us any guns.'

'No, of course not!'

'But we can get them from elsewhere.'

'Yes!'

'The lesson was driven home to me one day in Chipinga when I was at a filling station,' said Silas Mushonga. 'I was driving the Party's Volkswagen with the words in capital letters "ONE MAN, ONE VOTE!" A white man came round, looked at the slogan, shook his head, and then asked me, "But how are you going to get it?" I asked him, "Get what?" He said, "One Man, One Vote." I told him that we were organizing the people so that we get the majority. He sniffed in derision, and invited me to follow him to his car. Then he took out a rifle, and showed me, and then asked me the question, "Have you got this?" I said, "No." "Then you're just wasting your time," he said. I told him we had the people behind us. I got his point, though, and I've never forgotten it.'

'He couldn't have put it better,' said Gideon Masuku drily.

'This is why I'm so critical of the Son of the Soil who wants to have people behind him, when he should have guns behind him,' said Silas Mushonga. 'What he says would go down very well with the whites if he had guns behind him. When the guns speak, the white man listens. That is his mother tongue, and he readily understands it.'

'We have got to speak in his own language, not the English language which the Son of the Soil speaks so well, but the language of the gun,' added John Sibanda.

'Look at South Africa, what happens there?' Silas Mushonga asked himself a rhetorical question. 'The black people there have only 13 per cent of the land and the rest is European land. The blacks there outnumber the whites by four to one. What is the logic of this disproportionate land allocation? The logic is to be found nowhere else except in the gun. Look at the situation in this country: half the land is classified as African and the other half as European. There are six million blacks and only 250,000 whites! What is the logic of this land allocation? The gun. Nothing else. Its only justification is the gun. The gun means everything to the white man in Rhodesia and in South Africa. Therefore the gun must mean everything to the black man if he is to cope with the present situation. It's a gunpowder situation and it needs a gunpowder approach. Any other approach is naive and unrealistic.'

It was not that the four Sons of the Soil were bloodthirsty. They were desperate men—good men who had been driven to this position by the white man's ideology of white supremacy. They thirsted and hungered after freedom and independence in their own native land. They wanted more guns, and more of them, not to acquire other people's land, or to deprive other people of their rights, but to retrieve their own rights from the grasping hand of white supremacy. They wanted these guns for redemptive purposes. They wanted to redeem themselves from the clutches of white supremacy. They wanted both black and white to bleed to redeem the human status of the black man which had been trampled down by the white man. They would have done the same thing if the same thing had been done to them by another black man. But the question that now remained before them was, having agreed on their necessity, where to get these guns?

'We should forget all about Britain when it comes to the question of supplying weapons to the black man here,' began John Sibanda.

'And the United States too,' added Gideon Masuku.

'And France,' added Simon Mugadza.

'One might as well ask for weapons from South Africa!' jeered Silas Mushonga.

'None of these countries dare supply the black man here with the necessary weapons because directly and indirectly they are part and parcel of the white conspiracy against democracy. They also do not want it enjoyed by the black man here,' said John Sibanda. 'They are fellow conspirators with the whites here.'

'It's kith-and-kin politics,' observed Gideon Masuku.

'They will supply weapons to the white man here, but not to the black man,' said John Sibanda. 'If our plot against white supremacy is to succeed, we must get the full support of the Soviet Union, the People's Republic of China, and other Communist countries. They are interested in supplying us with weapons so that we can have majority rule here and do away with this white-minority dictatorship. Whatever the West may say, it cannot be gainsaid that the West strengthens the hand of dictatorship in this country, but the East strengthens the hand of democracy.'

'I can't see how the West can answer that one,' added Simon Mugadza.

'The best friend of democracy in this country is the Communist bloc,' agreed Gideon Masuku.

'You see, Sons of the Soil,' continued John Sibanda, 'why is the white man here so much afraid of Communism? It is because Communism stands *against* what the white man here stands *for*. If Communism tomorrow would side with the white-minority dictatorship, the white man here would be the first to praise it to the heavens. But because it condemns minority regimes in Southern Africa which oppress the majorities, they are scared of it.'

'Quite so,' the other three concurred.

'This is the black man's great hour of need,' said Silas Mushonga. 'He needs Communist help just as the West needed it in their heroic struggle against Nazism. We need it against white supremacy, and the West should appreciate our position.'

'If Communist help was good for them to combat Nazism,' observed Gideon Masuku, 'it is equally good for us in fighting white supremacy in this country.'

The four Sons of the Soil were unanimous that they would have to depend more and more on Communist countries if they were to meet effectively the bullet-power approach of the white man. But the next question that occupied their attention was how to get these weapons from the Communist countries which were so willing to help the black man in his noble cause of liberating his own country so that he might also reassert his human dignity like other men throughout God's good world. 'We committed no particular sin against God that we should be the dogs of other human beings,' all four men agreed.

'There's no point in asking our friends to send us the weapons here,' said John Sibanda, 'but we must send our own men to train there so that they will know how to use them. We want weapons we can use, not weapons we can't use.'

'It's a sad thing indeed,' said Gideon Masuku, 'that after living with these whites for all these years we still have not got closer together. One would have expected that after all these decades black and white would have struck an understanding, but no!'

'The impregnable wall of white supremacy will not allow any understanding to develop between black and white,' said Silas Mushonga. 'This is why the whole wall must be destroyed so that normal human intercourse will flow between black and white.'

'We must shoot down the wall, and that is why we need more bullet power,' said John Sibanda.

'Our plot against dictatorship must not fail. It must succeed. It is good for the black man here. And it is also good for the white man in the long run,' said Simon Mugadza.

6

Bishop Kupfava

Bishop Christopher Kupfava was in his middle 40s. He was a widely travelled man, and of a generous disposition towards all people regardless of the colour of their skin. He tried to interpret the Christian teachings as well as he could. He was in charge of a circuit whose African Christian membership ran into sixty thousand. When he first began his pastoral work, he was widely regarded by both black and white as a bridge between the two races. In that function he was supposed to interpret the blacks to the whites, and conversely the whites to the blacks. In theory this function seemed easy and feasible, but in practice it was an impossible task.

In the first place, did the white man really wish to understand the black man? Did the black man really wish to understand the white man? Did the people as people have to understand one another through some human interpreter like themselves? Wasn't understanding blacks or whites through the Bishop a waste of time, second-hand knowledge instead of first-hand knowledge? If the Bishop was interpreting overseas blacks and whites in Rhodesia, that would have been a realistic and necessary function. But why interpret to them people who live together in the same country? Why didn't such people find out more about one another themselves?

Between black and white there was a thick dividing wall of white supremacy ingeniously constructed by the white man himself so that the Bishop shuttled between the black side and the white side of the wall trying his pastoral best to interpret each side to the other. Could real understanding between the two races develop so long as there was this wall of white supremacy? At times the Bishop's function in this connection seemed a highly superficial one, and yet there it was in all sanity put down as one of his important functions as a Bishop!

The next thing which was a real problem for the Bishop was what to interpret. The what of his function was both important and necessary. What did the whites want the Bishop to interpret about them to the blacks? What did the blacks want him to interpret about them to the whites? Did the whites want him to convey to the blacks their demands of white supremacy? Did the blacks want him to convey to the whites their political aspirations? But how was the Bishop to convey these messages effectively unless the blacks and the whites had normal social intercourse? The Bishop was supposed to be a bridge, and a bridge is indifferent to what passes over it! In his function of interpreting the two races to each other, he ran the danger of identifying himself with one or the other race. He had to be noncommittal, but how could a man with a sensitive soul be noncommittal when at times there were acts on both sides which simply outraged the soul? As a rule, it is much easier to speak against the evil of the poor and weak, but most difficult to talk against the evil of the rich and powerful. The black man was powerless, and it was naturally easier to denounce his evil ways than those of the white man who was powerful. In other words, how was the Bishop to interpret the powerless to the powerful, and the powerful to the powerless? Was he to perform his function in terms of power or truth as he saw it? This placed the Bishop in a most unenviable position.

'Come in, Mr Hazel,' said the Bishop going to the door of his study to greet a visitor.

'Good morning to you, Bishop,' said Hazel, entering the clergyman's room and settling himself comfortably in a chair.

The conversation of the two men dwelt on the weather,

African education, juvenile delinquency, and low church attendance.

'I'm afraid, Bishop, that Dr Moyo is getting a bad name for himself among the whites around here,' said Hazel at last.

'Why?'

'He's becoming very political.'

'I see.'

'That's not what we expect of a well-educated African. He's one of us. We like him. But he'll soon lose our sympathy if he persists in his politics like that.'

'That would be a pity.'

'It's safer for him and his family to keep out of politics. After all, he's a well-educated man. He is not like one of these fellows who have never been able to make ends meet.'

'You know, Mr Hazel, politics is in the air these days.'

'Yes, Bishop, I do know. But I think you should advise him to keep out of it altogether.'

'Well, I'll certainly convey that to him when he calls around this evening.'

'Oh, he'll be here tonight? I wish you would, then. You see, Bishop, this matter of Dr Moyo is more serious than I have stated. You know very well that practically all our mission schools here depend upon the financial support of the whites. If Dr Moyo continues to antagonize the white community as he's doing at present, the whites will come to think that mission schools are bad places, and the whole mission work will collapse just like that! And thousands of African children will suffer, and many African teachers will be out of employment. No, Dr Moyo has to be more considerate than that. One man should not spoil things for all these people. He himself has had an excellent education, but now he wants to spoil the chances for others to get the same education.'

'I shall certainly convey your feelings to him when he shows up tonight.'

'Thanks, Bishop.'

Hazel left the Bishop's study, and the Bishop fell to

pondering. What was he to advise Dr Moyo? Suppose Dr Moyo withdrew from African nationalist politics, what would this really mean? Would this not mean his submission to white supremacy? In effect therefore it appeared to the Bishop's mind that to advise Dr Moyo to refrain from politics was tantamount to advising him to capitulate to white supremacy. And suppose he did advise him to do that, wouldn't Dr Moyo regard the Bishop as a white man's stooge? If, on the other hand, he did not advise him as requested, would he not, in the eyes of whites like Mr Hazel, be another Dr Moyo, and thereby jeopardize the finances of the mission schools which were attended by many thousands of African boys and girls?

Dr John Moyo arrived as expected that evening and was warmly welcomed by the Bishop. 'You have been away for almost three weeks,' he said.

'Quite.'

'What places did you touch this time?'

'Oh, many, Bishop. Bulawayo, Plumtree, Wankie, Gwanda, West Nicholson, Beit Bridge, Filabusi, Fort Rixon. Practically the whole of Matebeleland.'

'And the response?'

'Fabulous, Bishop. There can be no doubt that people in this country desire to rule themselves as in other African countries to the north of us. The people want to know when independence is coming.'

'Look here, John. Mr Hazel was here this morning. He says you are getting a bad name for yourself.'

'A bad name?'

'Because you go all over the shore doing politics. He asked me to advise you to leave politics alone.'

'Give up politics?'

'Yes.'

'Why?'

'Because if you continue in politics whites here will withdraw their financial support of our mission schools.'

'Did he really say that, Bishop?'

'Yes. He said it.'

'He doesn't quite understand how deeply committed I am to the liberation struggle. I've become wedded to it. He should know that by now. I left my job at the university for this very thing he expects me to give up for a good name among whites! Who cares anyway for a good name among them? We live in two entirely separate worlds. They are on the other side of the wall and we are on this side, and for me it is this side that matters.'

'I shall report to him accordingly.'

'Put a little more sting in what you have to tell him about what I have just told you.'

'That's none of my business, John. You know I'm just a conveyor belt in this respect.'

'You couldn't convey some of my sting?'

'Ha, ha, ha. No, I'm afraid.'

'I'm afraid, Bishop, I must go now. I've a meeting in Umtali in about an hour's time.'

Three days later, Robert Hazel called around the mission to hear Dr Moyo's reactions. The Bishop recounted his interview with Dr Moyo, and Hazel was evidently disappointed that Dr Moyo had not changed his mind. He had very little to say on that day, but as he drove back to Umtali where he lived he was in a state of some agitation.

'It's hard to understand the mind of a nigger,' he said to himself. 'We educate him, and our reward is that he deserts us to be with the other niggers!'

In his own mind the missions had failed hopelessly, and in one sense he was right. Many whites had expected the schools to turn out annually thousands of 'yes' men and women, but they completely overlooked the fact that education encourages the development of critical faculties, the fear of the Lord encourages the defiance of man, and that all in all the mission schools encouraged the freedom of the mind and the spirit, and these turned out to be the uncompromising enemies of white supremacy.

Meanwhile, four men had called on the Bishop. They were in their early 30s. They were disillusioned, bitter men, and they were highly critical of the whole Church. They had expected that if they prayed hard in church, God was going to hear their prayers. They had been brought up in the tradition that God does hear our prayers. They had therefore prayed for the independence of their country for a long time, but it had not come. Did God really hear their prayers? If He heard them, why had independence not come to their country? Were they praying for a wrong thing so that God deemed it unwise to give it to them? Like the children of Israel who believed that no ethical God would allow injustice or evil to triumph over righteousness, they had believed that, somehow or other, God would bring to an abrupt end the many injustices they were suffering at the hands of white supremacy. But apparently He had not done that, and so they had come to air their view before the Bishop.

'Bishop,' began the first man, 'why hasn't God answered our prayers for independence?'

'You are teaching us impossible things!' the second man said bitterly. ' "Blessed are the meek, for they shall inherit the earth." We are meek, but we have been disinherited of our land. When shall we inherit it?'

'I don't think that you are correct to say we are meek or humble,' the Bishop replied gently.

'What are we then?'

'We are a conquered people. A weak people.'

'And therefore humble.'

'No. Humility is an inner quality. The question of humility does not arise in a conquered, weak people. Only a free, independent people can be said to be humble or not humble, and when a people are free, independent, and humble they inherit the earth because they are guided in their national life by eternal values, and humility is one of these.'

'I see, Bishop,' said the man doubtfully.

'When you are humbled by hostile external circumstances, that's no particular virtue in you. You are not thereby humble, although you are humbled! Humility is an internal virtue which is part of our inner strength which helps us to inherit the earth.'

'But, Bishop, don't you think the Church is one of the strong arms of white supremacy?' asked the third man.

'What do you yourselves think?' counter-questioned the Bishop.

'We think it is,' cried the four men.

'Why do you think so?'

'I'll venture an answer, Bishop,' pleaded the fourth man.

'Go on.'

'Because the Church is so silent on the question of African independence, but it's clear and loud on white supremacy. There are so many priests, preachers, evangelists, and teachers always telling the black man to be humble, to borrow your phrase, when he is already humbled by the strong forces of white supremacy; to love the white man, when the white man doesn't want to see the black man near him! To be peaceful, when white supremacy is disturbing that peace; to be merciful, when white supremacy is merciless upon the black man; to be pure in heart, when white supremacy causes the heart of the black man to be so impure! Don't you think, Bishop, that instead of the Church constantly telling us this, this should be told to those who believe in white supremacy?'

'I might as well add, Bishop,' intervened the first man, 'that the Church seems to be more interested in preaching to the black man than to the white man. It is only interested in softening the hard blows of white supremacy, but not in eliminating them. One gathers the impression that the Church encourages white supremacy to keep itself in good business. The Church seems more interested in interpreting to the black man the required ways of white supremacy than the ways of God who has, in many instances, become the God of white supremacy.'

'Before you comment, Bishop,' said the second man, 'I also wish to add this. For almost a hundred years now, many

Churches in this country have accepted white supremacy as
the right thing. They have taught the black man the ways of
the white man, and the ways of the white man are the ways
of white supremacy, and these can't be the ways of God, you
see!'

'I take it that you now thoroughly dislike the Church. Am
I correct in this?'

'Yes, Bishop. You are correct.'

'You dislike it because you believe it teaches white supremacy. Is that right?'

'Yes, Bishop.'

'I now wish to put to you an important question. Suppose
the Church did not preach white supremacy, which you believe it does, would you dislike the Church?'

'No, of course not.'

'Would you dislike the beatitudes you have quoted to me?'

'Certainly not.'

'In other words, what you dislike with the Church is the
use to which it is put. Am I correct?'

'Yes, correct, Bishop.'

'In other words, you like what the Church as a religious
institution stands for, but you do not like the use to which it
is put. Am I correct?'

'Very much so, Bishop.'

'You feel that the Church should not serve the interests of
white supremacy. I entirely agree with you. It's a point I
shall take up with the Synod.'

'What we want to hear the Church say, Bishop, is this. If
the white man commits any of the evils of white supremacy,
let the Church speak up loud and clear. If the black man
commits evil, let the Church do the same thing. Evil is evil,
you see, Bishop, no matter who does it.'

7

Sons and Daughters of the Soil

'That's white supremacy on the wing,' said Titus Dlakama pointing to two jet fighters sweeping over the African townships.

'It's a show of power,' agreed George Kunesu.

'And you see those three Dakotas over Harare?' asked Titus Dlakama. 'This is what we call aerial political intimidation.'

'That's right,' agreed George Kunesu.

'You see those police trucks at Machipisa?' asked Titus Dlakama.

'So many of them coming and going,' remarked George Kunesu with some apprehension.

'That's white supremacy on the wheel,' quietly observed Titus Dlakama.

'I wonder if they are expecting trouble at the meeting today?' wondered George Kunesu.

'Not quite that. They want to frighten the Sons and Daughters away from the meeting so that it becomes a total failure. Who knows if these power-paraders have not received orders from higher authority to deliberately provoke trouble as an excuse for shooting down a few black men to impress the survivors that the black man must at all times give way to white supremacy? How often have I been told by the police, "We have been given orders to kill," when they are investigating ordinary political cases!'

'Oh, here they come. I hope they won't ask us for our passes.'

Three police jeeps passed by, each loaded with eight policemen and police reservists, and, except for the driver, each held a rifle. They did not speak to Titus Dlakama and George Kunesu. They seemed only interested in intimidating from afar. After ten minutes another convoy of three jeeps went past them.

This was at only 8 a.m. on Sunday morning, but the meeting was due to be held at 2 p.m. at Chaminuka Square, Highfield, Salisbury. Delegates from all the fifty districts were expected to attend it, and because of this, arrangements had been made that each district should send at least one busload of delegates. The districts that were farthest from Salisbury managed to send only one busload, but others sent two, and those nearest sent between three and five busloads. This was to be a national rally which had been widely publicized and throughout the country there had been great excitement about it. Some came to the rally by private cars, and others by open trucks, and one had a feeling that great issues were going to be settled at this rally!

The white government was naturally apprehensive that blacks from all over the country were going to converge on Salisbury to hear their own black leaders. Strict orders were given to the police in every district to stop buses, private cars, and open trucks that were proceeding to Salisbury, and check the efficiency of the brakes in the interest of public safety! As the police faithfully carried out this order, it became clear that only African-driven vehicles carrying black passengers were subjected to this exercise. One bus, for instance, from Beit Bridge, carrying eighty passengers, was stopped and brake-checked ten times before discharging its passengers at Highfield. On their way back home, however, after the meeting, not a single one of them was required to stop and to have the brakes tested for efficiency in the interest of public safety!

Although these orders were very provocative, the district organizers had given strict instructions to their people that they should co-operate as well as they could with the police and not provoke them so that they would get detained by the police on this or that charge, and thus fail to get to the big rally. In most cases, the police failed completely to provoke the delegates to the big rally. There were a few exceptions which resulted in the detention of a few individuals but for all practical purposes, the police failed. Almost 99.9 per cent of all the delegates had their *situpas*, or identity cards, or travelling passes, so the police had no good excuse to detain them.

As the hour-hand moved towards 1 o'clock, people began to converge on Chaminuka Square. People from Mabvuku, Tafara, Harare, Mufakose, Kambuzuma, and from the city centre drove there, but others from nearer places walked, while quite a sizeable number cycled. As the hour-hand moved towards 2 o'clock, the numbers had swollen to almost 15,000 people, and by 2 p.m., by police count, it was estimated at more than 25,000 people.

There were the Zezurus, Karangas, Manyikas, Ndaus, Korekores, Nhanzwas, Tongas, Ndebeles, Vendas, Sothos, Chewas, Angonis, Hungwes, Bembas, Lozis, Budyas, and a good sprinkling of other tribes. In fact, it was a vast medley of tribes who spoke different languages and different dialects, but who spoke the same language of African freedom and independence, and who spoke the same dialect of human dignity. They were different tribes, but white supremacy oppressed and suppressed them alike, and they reacted alike against it. White supremacy had managed unwittingly to unite them against itself, and hence, they all came to the big rally chanting, 'One man, one vote!' and 'Independence Now!'

There were men and women, and boys and girls of all ages. For a while, age and sex were buried as men and women, and boys and girls shouted in Shona: '*Nyika yedu!* This is our country!'

In attendance at this rally were black soldiers, policemen, prison warders, nurses, teachers, trade unionists, taxi drivers, bus drivers, truck drivers, tractor drivers, cooks, waiters, tailors, salesmen, travel agents, firemen, train drivers, accountants, clerks, court interpreters, ministers of religion, evangelists, preachers, builders, carpenters, agricultural demonstrators, farmers, dip-attendants, witchdoctors. They pursued different professions, trades, and other occupations, but they pursued only one and the same political goal, namely, Majority Rule Now! They desired the wind of change to blow away from their land white supremacy which had polluted their air, fouled the courts of justice, embittered human relations between black and white, perverted highly treasured religious values, and desecrated and distorted humanity. They had all come to the big rally to hear black leaders speak the soul of the black man—a third-rate citizen in his own country, a beggar in his native land, a stranger in his fatherland. They had come to find out if their leaders really understood their sufferings. They had come to find out if their leaders knew where they were leading the people. It was *their* rally, and *their* leaders were going to speak to them about *their* own country. It was a great day for most of them. 'One man, one vote!' they chanted as they waited.

Behind the huge crowd were fifteen screened police jeeps and about a hundred policemen and police reservists all armed; but the people ignored them. There were five police dogs, all well trained in scaring away Africans. They were all under leash. In front of the huge crowd was a large table on which two detectives in plain clothes placed their recorder so that every word the speakers uttered could be accurately recorded for further examination by the police after the big rally. The purpose of this examination was to check if any words so uttered in the hearing of the 25,000 people infringed any section of the Law and Order (Maintenance) Act. If the police were satisfied that a section of the Act had been contravened, then an appropriate court action would be taken against whoever had uttered such words. There was a microphone into which every speaker had to speak so that his voice could be properly recorded.

James Kunzekwayedza was the chairman of the meeting. He was assisted by three other members of the Highfield branch of the People's Party. The Highfield youth helped with seating the people on the ground who jubilantly sang, '*Tinoda Zimbabwe*'—'We love Zimbabwe'—as they waited for the Sons of the Soil who were to address them that afternoon.

'They've come!' cried Chairman James Kunzekwayedza.

Great silence descended on the great crowd. Hearts beat faster. Eyes looked for them, and, indeed, there they were!

'Sons of the Soil! Sons of the Soil!' the people roared.

They were now wildly cheering, whistling, and ululating, and repeating, 'One man, one vote!' and shouting, '*Nyika yedu*!'

The three Sons of the Soil who had just arrived used the Black Power salute in acknowledging this most arousing welcome, and the people soon followed suit. They took their seats at the big table, and people sat on the ground in great expectation. They were already on the Mount of Transfiguration even before the Sons of the Soil had spoken to them. A mountain-top experience had already begun and would probably continue for the next three hours. The mere sight of so many people with one common desire among them—INDEPENDENCE—was in itself an exciting, exhilarating, elevating, and rejuvenating experience. Even the three Sons of the Soil who had just arrived could not escape the highly expectant mood of the people. Their hearts also beat faster in tune with those of the 25,000. The chairman introduced the three Sons of the Soil, and the 25,000 cheered and applauded.

The first speaker was Simon Matambanadzo. He was about 40, tall, and of a massive build. He spoke for about twenty-five minutes. His voice was deep but clear, and carried well. He dwelt mostly on how the black man in the country had trusted absolutely the word of the white man, and how he had now changed from absolute trust to absolute distrust. He wound up by saying:

'In the past, when the white man first came to our country, which he has now made his, we had no reason to distrust him. We took him at his word. But now we have every reason to distrust him, and distrust him completely because he has let us down. [*Loud cheers and applause.*] We were very foolish to trust him in the first place, because trust, among all people, is a result of a certain quality of behaviour. What this country needs today is not trust between black and white, but fair dealing between them, and it is this fair dealing which will establish trust. We desire no trust but actions of fair dealing with regard to land allocation, employment opportunities, and education. When the white man discriminates against us because we are black, that is not fair dealing, and we can only get a square deal in this country provided we have majority rule now!'

The next speaker was Josiah Mkhwananzi. He was in his early 50s, stockily built, and was obviously not a stranger to the art of orating to big crowds. He let the crowd carry him, but he also carried it with him. He spoke for about thirty minutes. His delivery and argument were brilliant and convincingly embellished right through with political wit and penetrating insights.

'It is imperative for all of us to remember this,' he said, 'that we are our own liberators. No country can liberate us but ourselves. [*Cheers and applause.*] If we are liberated by others, then the country will belong to our liberators, and not to us. [*Wild cries of 'Son of the Soil!' 'Action Now!' Prolonged whistling and cheering.*] God is not going to send his angels to do the job for us, but we ourselves must do the job. We must be prepared, as Ben Bella once stated in 1963 in Addis Ababa, to die a little. To die a little, Sons and Daughters of the Soil, that is the whole secret of national liberation. No dying a little, no freedom and independence, and this must never be allowed to happen! It is given to man to fight, and fight, and fight to liberate himself. Better to die fighting for the liberation of our country than to die a natural death.'

There were wild cheers, whistling, and ululation, then spontaneously the whole crowd broke into the militant strains of '*Tinoda Zimbabwe*' and as the enormous crowd chorussed '*Hondo!*'—'War!'—the whole atmosphere became supercharged with martial music and the police and police reservists and the police dogs became more alert than ever. Soon the excitement died down. The martial music died in the distance, and Josiah Mkhwananzi resumed his seat.

The last and chief speaker was Dr John Moyo, President of the People's Party. He was aware that the audience was in a receptive mood, and he felt himself at his very best.

'Sons and Daughters of the Soil!' he began, and loud cheers and applause at the very address rose into the air.

The way he said 'Sons and Daughters of the Soil!' was loaded with meaning. It was packed with warmth towards his people; it rang with affectionate feeling for them; it rang with deep and sincere concern for their miserable lot; it established a spontaneous we-feeling between himself and them; it raised their high spirits still higher; it gave them a feeling of having a true national leader. This was now to be their climax on the Mount of Transfiguration. For almost two minutes the Son of the Soil could not begin his speech, but he waited until the excitement of the 25,000 had died down. Then he began again, 'Sons and Daughters of the Soil! We meet here today not as free men and women of our own country, but as an oppressed people, strangers in our own country, a people whose fundamental rights and freedoms are abridged by other men like ourselves, and the presence here of armed police, armed police reservists, and police dogs bears evidence to that fact. Even dogs have been trained to interfere with our rights and freedoms!'

Cries of 'Shame! Shame!' ran through the audience.

'We are treated in our own fatherland as third-rate people. The white man rates himself in this country as first, the Coloureds and Asians as second, and the black man as third. In other words, he rates his own humanity as 100 per cent; that of Coloureds and Asians as $66\frac{2}{3}$ per cent; and that of the black man as 33⅓. The humanity of the African in this country is rated the lowest.'

'Shame! Shame!' cried the 25,000.

'In everything in this our God-given country, we are given only a third of the normal value of things. Citizenship?' he asked.

'Third-rate!' they roared.

'Housing?'

'Third-rate!'

'Wages and salaries?'

'Third-rate!'

'Jobs?'

'Third-rate!'

'Education?'

'Third-rate!'

'Land?'

'Third-rate!'

'Water supply?'

'Third-rate!'

'All services?'

'Third-rate!'

'That's the absolute truth about the position of the black man in this country. This is so because of only one thing in this country, and that is the white man's ideology of white supremacy which treats the black man as a thing at the disposal of the white man. The worst enemy—our deadliest enemy—is white supremacy with all that it has meant to us!'

'Down with it! Down with it!' cried the 25,000.

'It is an evil of evils which we must exterminate from our country root, stem, and branch. For almost a hundred years now it has polluted our political atmosphere, fouled justice, dehumanized humanity, trampled underfoot the rights of the black man, deprived him of the opportunity to earn according to his ability, and has sown seeds of suspicion, distrust, and fear between black and white; and from day to day, week to week, month to month, year to year, and from decade to decade, white supremacy has worked ceaselessly for the subjection of the black man in his own native land!'

There were prolonged cheers, applause, whistling, and ululation.

'Tell me now. What is it that causes the vote to be denied to the black man in this country?'

'White supremacy!' roared back the 25,000.

'Correct. Take away white supremacy and every black adult would have a vote today. White supremacy is the most selfish ideology that has ever appeared under the canopy of heaven. The black soldier is good enough to defend and die for this country, but he is not good enough to vote. The black policeman is good enough to keep law and order in this country, but he is not good enough to vote. The black prison warder is good enough to look after prisoners, but he is not good enough to vote. The black teacher is good enough to educate and train boys and girls who are the citizens and workers of tomorrow, but he is not good enough to vote. The black farmer is good enough to produce on land, but he is not good enough to vote. The black transport operator is good enough to keep transport going, but he is not good enough to vote. That's how white supremacy works! Double standard always!'

'Down with it! Down with it!' they cried.

The militant young men and women shook angry fists in the air as if trying to show the police and police reservists what was in store for their ideology of white supremacy. Some cried 'Action!' Some 'Shame!' Some '*Nyika yedu!*' Some 'These white ——!' To a man, they felt the white man in denying them the vote, did them great injustice. John Moyo's oratorical wizardry had buoyed them up to the very top of the Mount of Transfiguration, and from that vantage-point they saw themselves in a new light. They saw their own country in a new perspective. They felt deeply. They thought deeply. They reacted strongly.

Then John Moyo castigated the Law and Order (Maintenance) Act. He asserted that this Act was designed first and foremost to frustrate African political organization, to distort and break African political unity, and above all to muzzle, destroy, abort, weaken, and adulterate African political opinion. To the great cheers of the 25,000, he labelled it the White Supremacy (Maintenance) Act! Then he moved on to the Immorality and Indecency Act. He skilfully lampooned, derided, and mocked it, and to the accompaniment of wild cheers, he called it an immoral and indecent Act! Then he moved on to the allocation of land between black and white, and pointed out that to divide the land equally between 6,000,000 blacks and 250,000 whites and call that equality and therefore justice and fair dealing between black and white, was unpardonable hypocrisy, and a criminal act, a crass repudiation of justice and fair play, a thorn in the flesh of every black man, and a challenge the black man had to meet without flinching for one moment!

'All roads in Rhodesia lead to the Citadel of White Supremacy,' he declared. 'Why is there no equal pay for equal work in this country?'

'White supremacy!' the crowd roared back.

'Why are the black people being moved away from their traditional places?'

'White supremacy!'

'Why are the Tangwena tribe being driven away from their traditional homes?'

'White supremacy!'

'Why are the blacks at Epworth Mission being threatened with eviction from this mission land?'

'White supremacy!'

'Why can't blacks own property in our cities and towns?'

'White supremacy!'

'Why can't they be allowed to run business there?'

'White supremacy!'

'The whites here will tell you that the biggest danger facing this country is Communism. Is that true?'

'No!'

'What is it?'

'White supremacy!'

'That's right! White supremacy—that evil ideology begotten of Satan himself—which sets man against man just
because they happen to be different in the colour of their
skin! That evil ideology whose very soul is stone and concrete, insensitive, unresponsive to the best things in human
relations....'

'Shame! Shame!' cried the crowd. 'Down with it! Down
with it!'

'What are courts in this country but rubber-stamps of injustice? Can anyone deny that? Under the unholy umbrella
of white supremacy, no court can escape the function of being a rubber-stamp of injustice. They cannot possibly administer justice. That would be impossible. Under such
circumstances, therefore, magistrates and judges are servants
of injustice and not justice. They are paid fat salaries for the
administration of injustice and not justice. The injustice is
in the law, and therefore, since the courts administer the law,
they administer injustice. Hence, under such circumstances,
the Chief Justice becomes the Chief Injustice! The police
have no alternative but to enforce injustice since the law
itself contains it as required by white supremacy.'

The crowd cheered wildly. It was clear that the natural
eloquence of the Son of the Soil, the force of his argument, his
firm grasp of the sufferings of the black man, his outspoken-
ness, and above all, his dedication and devotion to the cause
of the Sons and Daughters of the Soil moved them to the
very core of their being. His words had broken loose the
chains around their souls. They had unshackled their minds
and kindled fierce flames of freedom in their hearts. They had
injected more strength into their muscles. They had lifted
a downtrodden, third-rate people out of the valley of de-
pression, dejection, pessimism, and near-lifelessness to the
very top of the Mount of Transfiguration where breezes of
freedom, hope, optimism, and jubilation blew as if pro-
nouncing a benediction upon their troubled souls. A vision
of a new Zimbabwe where man is man regardless of the
colour of his skin spread before their eyes, and they caught a

glimpse of Paradise. They had become lost to the real world and the real world had become lost to them. The transported 25,000 for the first time collectively felt they were captains of their own souls and masters of their own destiny. They broke into the martial strains of '*Tinoda Zimbabwe*' and with thunderous gusto chorussed '*Hondo!*'

Was it '*Hondo!*' to bring about the new Paradise on earth which the oratorical wizardry of the Son of the Soil had spread before their eyes? It was difficult to say. Was it '*Hondo!*' to express the exuberance of their new elation? Most likely it was. Or was it a conscious or unconscious desire to unite in song and hence in their determined struggle against white supremacy? It probably was. Whatever it was, the 25,000 were having a mountain-top experience which was broader than the bigotry, more ennobling than the degradation, more redemptive than the destruction of human values, and far more universal than the uncompromising particularism of white supremacy. Yes, it was a mountain-top experience never to be forgotten as long as those who went through it lived.

Then one policeman approached the chairman and told him that there was to be no singing of that song again! Hardly had he finished speaking than some militant youths shouted, 'Don't spoil our meeting, you white pig!' And when the policeman addressed his attention to the militants by way of asserting the white man's authority, like hungry hounds they fell upon him, and confusion and disorder started. Four shots were fired into the crowd. Tear gas was thrown. Some young militants rushed upon the police jeeps. Stones and bottles descended upon the police and police reservists while tear-gas canisters and a few bullets landed among the crowd. Men and women ran away in every direction. Five helicopters appeared in the sky and dropped more tear-gas canisters on the various groups so as to prevent any regrouping. The 1st Battalion, which had been surrounding Highfield since that morning, but which had kept away from the meeting, moved in with loaded sub-machine-guns. There were about 1,000 of them. More police and army reinforcements poured into Highfield. The whole township was teeming with soldiers and policemen and police reservists. Stoning and shooting went on for almost an hour before the trouble came to an end. Chaminuka Square had not a single soul around except the police and the soldiers. The big rally had abruptly come to a close an hour ahead of time.

Thirty-five blacks had been shot dead; 10 white policemen and police reservists had been killed; all the police dogs had perished; 367 blacks had been seriously injured, 672 not so seriously wounded; 20 policemen and police reservists seriously injured and 30 slightly hurt; 10 police jeeps had been set on fire. Over 700 people were arrested as a result of the riot.

Thus the contest of bullet power and numerical strength —democratic power—came to an end with the latter unceremoniously dispersed, but to regroup in future to pursue the struggle to its logical conclusion determined by the overwhelming superiority of numbers and supported, if possible, by bullet power in the hands of the blacks.

8

Stand Firm!

The local papers carried the news of the big rally. It was on the front page of most newspapers. The national radio and TV also carried it, and soon it spread throughout the country like a wild fire, and provoked many lively discussions among both blacks and whites.

The Lamberts were to be found among the whites throughout the country.

'The police did a good job,' commented Roger Dixon. 'It's high time the black man was shown his proper place.'

'He's been forgetting it,' agreed Dan Hogg. 'But now he'll know who the boss is in this country.'

'If only one of the bullets could have strayed into the witchdoctor, that would have done it,' said Dixon regretfully.

'Mark you, I don't like the fact that ten white men were killed by these niggers,' said Hogg frowning, and with more white seriousness taking charge of him. 'Ten white men killed by niggers! Wild niggers! This is what gets me.'

'I agree. This should not have been allowed to happen. It's bad!'

To both Hogg and Dixon what was wrong in the whole sorry episode was not that ten policemen had been killed on duty, but that ten *white* men had been killed, and killed by blacks! Their emphasis was on *white*. *White*, and not so much policemen or persons, had been killed, and to make it worse, *white* had been killed by *black*! This fact troubled them and their kind. That *white* had killed *black* did not bother them in the slightest because this was only natural. It was generally accepted among whites that killing blacks for political reasons was a practical method of keeping the blacks in their place, and of reasserting the dominant role of the whites.

'And killing all five police dogs there! Absolutely unbelievable!' exclaimed Hogg with fury shooting out of his eyes.

'It's bad, when you come to think of it. The police were grossly inefficient. I can't forgive them! This must never be allowed to happen again!'

'A nigger even dares to kill a white man's dog! Damn it all, we've got to do something drastic, and pretty soon too!'

As the two men talked thus backwards and forwards about the five police dogs which perished in the struggle between black and white on Sunday, it was clear that their sympathies were with the canine species and not with the thirty-five dead blacks! The five police dogs were not ordinary dogs. They were the canine incarnation of white supremacy! Hence they got nearly as much sympathy as the ten *white* policemen who had died in the full harness of white supremacy.

'I didn't particularly like the idea of police helicopters flying over those nigger townships dropping tear-gas canisters. They should have dropped real bombs instead!' regretted Hogg.

'Yes, indeed. That would have driven the lesson home,' agreed Dixon.

'A few bombs dropped over all African townships throughout the country would really get the message right through the country in a matter of a day,' said Hogg.

'You are right. I really can't see how the white man can live in this country and remain its ruler unless the niggers here are made to fear him,' wondered Dixon. 'Remove the fear of the white from the niggers, and we are done for.'

'You couldn't be more right, Roger. The whole secret of ruling this country is fear. There's no need to beat about the bush. We must be realistic about it so that we don't confuse issues like so many of us.'

'Right, right.'

'I don't give a damn about democracy when it comes to these niggers. They are all niggers including their learned witchdoctor. And these wild niggers are crazy enough to think they can rule! They all must be ruled by the white man. There are no two ways about it.'

In stressing the element of fear as the genius of white rule in Rhodesia, the two white men were right. How else could a mere 250,000 whites rule 6,000,000 blacks! Freedom for these black millions would naturally liquidate white minority rule. Fear was thus the white man's only way of surviving politically. The police force, the army, the prison service, the civil service, the air force, and the like had therefore to strike deep fear in the heart of the black man so that he remained rulable for all time. This was the plain logic of white supremacy which the whites had to admit to themselves.

But not all the whites felt this way. There were some who deeply regretted the whole episode which had led to loss of human life.

'It is impossible to believe that what has been reported in the papers, over the air, and on TV, actually happened in this country,' said Mrs Ivy Duncan in real distress.

'Impossible!' exclaimed her husband. 'Why did the police have to provoke the people like that? Here are people unarmed. They are singing, just singing, and they have been singing since 1890. Then a bully policeman tells them to stop singing. And there's trouble. Can you blame the African?'

'Of course not,' replied Ivy. 'It was so tactless, so stupid to do such a thing!'

'To any fool it should have been obvious that the Africans gathered there had gathered there to air their grievances against the white man, and mark well, Ivy, the African has a genuine grievance against the white man in this country. But out comes a bully policeman to tell them not to air their grievances in a particular song which they had been singing even before the rally began. What could one expect from such provocative action?'

'Trouble of course!'

'And there was plenty of it, and the taxpayer has to pay for the crass stupidity of the police. When will they ever learn that these people are people like ourselves?'

'I wonder, Richard, if the white man here will ever learn anything! He seems to have ceased thinking rationally.'

'I am very much afraid, Ivy, that the white man in this country will never learn anything about Africans until he has gone through real trouble.'

'Yes, I fear so.'

'Now ten policemen are dead. Thirty-five people are also dead. Reason? Police stupidity. No policeman could have behaved like that if it had been a white audience, except in Nazi Germany. White policemen here behave towards the African people like tin gods. They are masters when they should be the servants of the public. They should have prevented crime by not interfering with the meeting. But they caused several crimes by sheer interference which was quite uncalled for.'

'If the white man is thinking he can deny the African freedom by shooting him down, then he's already fighting a losing battle.'

'It would be better, Ivy, for the white man to come to terms with the African now.'

'Quite right, Richard.'

Mr and Mrs Duncan were concerned with Rhodesia as a country not only for the white man, but for all those who lived in it. To them what mattered was not *white* or *black*, but human beings. The loss of human life was what particularly shocked them. But in condemning the tactlessness of the policeman who provoked the trouble, it did not seem to occur to them that tact was inconceivable in a situation in which even the police were taught that any black man, regardless of his age and educational status, was his natural inferior. They both forgot that every black man was required to say 'Sir' to every white man. Tact is usually a quality that is found between equals. Between black and white there was no equality of any kind. The white man was supposed to order the black man who was in turn supposed to obey the order without question. This was always the meaning of white supremacy in practical situations involving black and white. In behaving as he did, the policeman who provoked a riot at the big rally was acting according to the expectations of white supremacy—namely, the white man orders, and the black man obeys because the white man has ordered him!

In the Salisbury African townships, the riot had also sparked off heated discussions.

'I hope what happened at the rally has opened his eyes,' began Simon Simango. 'He's a little too academic!'

'I hope it did,' said Jesse Chinamano.

'He's too reasonable in dealing with the whites,' complained Simon Simango. 'I hope some of that tear gas found its way into his eyes to open them a little wider.'

'That would do him a world of good,' agreed Jesse Chinamano.

'He needs something like what happened at the rally to convince him that this is not the time for tongues but for bullets to speak. Everything has its own season.'

'Quite right.'

'This is a season for bullets, and the white man made his point very well.'

'He spoke in bullets in season,' affirmed Chinamano, 'and that's what the black man must also do. There's time to talk, and there's time to act. The white man knows when to talk, and he knows when to act, and he got his point across very effectively! But poor Son of the Soil doesn't seem to know when to talk, and when to act.'

'I cannot believe that he's a coward, so that he's afraid of real dynamic action,' said Simango.

'No,' negated Chinamano, 'anyone who knows the Son of the Soil well, cannot honestly say cowardice is one of his weaknesses. He's no chicken, you know!'

'Yes, but why this abdication of action, and dedication to talk, talk, talk?'

'It puzzles me too,' said Chinamano, shaking his head. Then he added, 'It would have been a bad show if only blacks had been killed at the rally!'

'Quite right, Son of the Soil. The white man must be left in no doubt that he is not the only one with power to kill, but the black man has also the same power. I like what happened on Sunday. The whites also died. Indeed, more blacks did die, but from our point of view the whites also did die!'

'That's the point.'

'You see, Son of the Soil, the black man showed that he also had killing power, and ten whites actually died! And I feel it is a good thing that the black man is now also prepared to kill the whites if they start killing the blacks wantonly. You cannot stop wanton killing of the blacks by not killing the whites! It is only killing in kind that will stop the whites.'

'I'm afraid that is the hard truth.'

'Take the question of the U.S.A. as a superpower. It would endanger the peace of the world, and the freedom of other countries, if the U.S.A. was the only superpower. But now there are two superpowers and China is in the making, and these two countries are very careful the way they control the enormous killing power at their disposal. There's real respect between the U.S.A. and the Soviet Union because they possess the same thing, and the world benefits generally.'

'I can see where you are leading to. Go on.'

'Because in this country only the white man has what the black man has not, there's no mutual respect between the two races. This is why it's damn important that we have more bullet power to speak on equal terms with the white man here.'

'I hope this lesson was forcefully driven home to the puzzling mind of the Son of the Soil.'

Throughout their conversation, these two men did not seem concerned with the fact that so much human life had been lost. They accepted this as something that was to be expected under such circumstances. They were more keenly

interested in what effect it would have on the relations between black and white. They were satisfied that the black
man had at long last awakened to the fact that he must kill
the whites to stop them killing the blacks. This, more than
anything else, pleased them. They saw it as evidence of the
growth of black power against the white man.

But some blacks busied themselves with the answers to the
question: why did the police provoke the trouble? They
were quite sure it was the police who provoked the trouble,
and not the militant black youths. They argued that the
militants merely reacted to police provocation.

'You see,' said Takawira, 'since Sunday morning the
police wanted to cause trouble in Highfield before the meeting so that they could call it off.'

'Do you think so?' asked Pfumojena.

'Oh, yes,' asserted Takawira. 'At Machipisa Shopping
Centre, for instance, the police were telling people to remember that this was a white man's country, and no baboon
would be allowed to rule it. If any baboon wanted to do that,
he could go to the mountains. Those were the only suitable
places for baboon rule!'

'Really!'

'I heard it with my own ears. And the police were really
disappointed that 25,000 people turned up in spite of everything they could do.'

'About that there can be no doubt.'

'You see, Son of the Soil,' continued Takawira, 'that meeting was a great success up to the point of the trouble. The
message of the Son of the Soil was coming through very
clearly, and it had seized the people. Everyone without exception felt the reality of Black Power.'

'It was a wonderful experience for me, you know!' con-
fessed Pfumojena. 'Absolutely wonderful!'

'The police felt it too. And what must have worried them
was that all the fifty districts had been represented by at

least eighty delegates each. The police were worried by the fact that after the rally these delegates would return to their respective districts with one message only: the message of Black Power.'

'I see,' nodded Pfumojena appreciatively.

'Somewhere along the line, the police had to intervene to show that Black Power after all wasn't that much of power! It wasn't that they thought there was going to be any trouble from the blacks. They knew very well that the blacks unarmed as they were dared not cause any trouble since the police would not hesitate to shoot them down.'

'Yes, I can see that.'

'But they also knew how to provoke us—especially the young militants. They wanted the delegates to carry the message back to their home districts that the white man kills, but of course this misfired since the other message will now be that the black man kills whites also! But if no white man were killed, then their message would have much more weight.'

'That's an interesting way of looking at it.'

'Now the delegates have two messages: Black Power and white power, and to all blacks, Black Power means a lot more than white power. The delegates actually saw Black Power in action against white power. This gave them hope that if they organize better they should be able to defeat white power. Most of those fellows had never seen blacks fighting whites with such determination. It was an eye-opener!'

Three days after the Sunday riot, John Moyo presided over an urgent meeting of the Central Committee of the People's Party, which comprised twenty-one members. The purpose of this meeting was to see what next the Party should do in the light of what had happened at the rally.

'The main point, Sons of the Soil,' said John Moyo, 'is that the meeting came to an abrupt close, an hour too soon, and this made it impossible for me to tell the people what we had arranged they should be told.'

'It was a good opportunity we were forced to miss,' replied someone from the Central Committee.

'Indeed, the opportunity was missed, so we must follow the people to their various districts as quickly as we can. There's no other way we can do this but to go there ourselves.'

A lengthy discussion followed on how best this could be done. The Committee was unanimous that John Moyo should not participate in this exercise but should remain in Salisbury so that the police should not have their suspicions aroused by his movements especially after the riot. The Committee felt that John Moyo should give the false impression that he was in Salisbury licking his wounds after the big rally! Each member of the Central Committee was assigned to two or three districts, and was to report back in person in two weeks time.

The purpose of these visits was to reassure the various supporters throughout the country that in spite of what the enemy had done at the rally, the Party had not yielded or flinched an inch. In fact, it was even more determined to wage the battle against the white man. The physical presence of the members of the Committee in the fifty districts would have the desired effect, whereas their absence, it was felt, would have an opposite one. They were to tell the people to stand firm, and never yield an inch of their ground. 'Stand firm!' was to be their watchword. There were other things which they were to explain to the people, but this watchword was to be the central message on which future action depended. The entire Committee had met in a most militant mood, and the district-visiting members carried it with them wherever they went for the next two weeks.

Here were black and white who had lived in the same country for almost a century, but were divided by a thick wall. On the white side of the wall, the white man was amassing bullet power, and on the black side, the black man was doing the same thing. The white man was calling for more military training, more police reservists, more army reservists, more informers and spies to deal effectively with what was going on on the black side of the wall. On the other hand, the black man was calling for more blacks to go abroad for military training wherever they could get it so that they could deal effectively with what was going on on the white side of the wall. Black and white literally besieged each other. If the black man had submitted soul, heart, and mind to white supremacy, the problem would have been quickly solved. The black man, therefore, had the answer to the problem between black and white in Rhodesia. Black submission was the answer, but would they submit? This was the question, and the white man set out to secure black submission by hook or by crook, but could he secure it? If, on the other hand, the white man gave up in thought, word, and deed his ideology of white supremacy, the problem, again, would have been immediately solved. The white man, therefore, had the answer to the problem between black and white. White repudiation of white supremacy was the answer, but would they do that? This was the question, and the black man had set out to force the white man by any means to repudiate white supremacy, but could he? And so the Central Committee of the People's Party sent out a clear message throughout the country: Stand firm! Against what? For what? These questions the devoted members of the Central Committee patiently explained on the black side of the wall.

9

The Rubber-Stamps of Injustice

'Silence in court!'

The people in court stood up, and in came a senior magistrate looking stiff and grave.

Some of the 700 people arrested during the riot were being tried on various charges under the Law and Order (Maintenance) Act. The magistrate's court at Harare was busy trying these men in groups and individually. But those arrested for the killing of the ten policemen and police reservists were indicted in the High Court. There were 40 of them. The 367 people who had been seriously injured were detained in hospital and were all facing police charges on the assumption that their being seriously wounded meant that they were causing trouble although most of them had sustained serious injuries while running away from trouble! They had collided with bullets and stones while fleeing! So they faced court trial after they recovered from their wounds. Most of the 672 slightly injured men and women did not go to hospital or clinic for fear of handing themselves over to the police, since their injuries would be taken to mean that they too had caused trouble during the riot. No one was indicted for the killing of the 35 blacks! This was because the State, through its police, had done the killing. But to the blacks, this distinction did not occur! It was simply whites killing blacks! The State was white and not black! It was simply what was expected to be done by the first-rate citizens to the third-rate citizens.

In Court No. 7 in the City Centre, Simon Matambanadzo

was facing a charge which would send him to jail for a maximum period of five years. The charge arose from his speech at the rally. His words were: 'But now we have every reason to distrust him, and distrust him completely.' According to the Law and Order (Maintenance) Act, such words were 'likely to cause disaffection between the races' and, therefore, to undermine the peace of the state.

In Court No. 10 Josiah Mkhwananzi was facing a charge which could send him to jail for a maximum period of ten years. The charge arose from his speech at the rally. The words were: 'We must be prepared . . . to die a little. . . . No dying . . . no freedom. . . . Better to die fighting for the liberation of our country than to die a natural death. . . .' These words, it was said, proposed violence and therefore contravened a section of the Law and Order (Maintenance) Act.

In Court No. 15, John Moyo was facing eight charges arising from his speech at the rally, and he faced a possibility of a maximum total of forty years! The prosecutor read out the charges against John Moyo:

'The accused contravened sections of the Law and Order (Maintenance) Act indicated in the charge sheet in that at a public gathering at Chaminuka Square, Highfield, Salisbury, he uttered the following words in the hearing of about 25,000 people there gathered:

'Count 1: "Even dogs have been trained to interfere with our rights and freedoms, and they have been actually brought here to do just that."

'Count 2: "The white man rates his own humanity as 100 per cent; that of Coloureds and Asians as 66⅔ per cent; and that of the black man as 33⅓ per cent."

'Count 3: "White supremacy is an evil which we must exterminate from our country root, stem, and branch."

'Count 4: "The Law and Order (Maintenance) Act is in fact a White Supremacy (Maintenance) Act. . . . It is begotten of Satan."

'Count 5: "What are courts but rubber-stamps of injustice? . . . Courts administer injustice . . . they cannot possibly administer justice."

'Count 6: "Magistrates and judges are servants of injustice . . . they are paid for the administration of injustice and not justice."

'Count 7: "The Chief Justice is in fact the Chief Injustice."

'Count 8: "The police . . . enforce injustice." '

'Do you plead guilty or not guilty?' asked the magistrate.

'Not guilty, Your Worship,' answered John Moyo.

'To all of them?' asked the magistrate.

'To all of them, Your Worship.'

The Crown witnesses gave evidence to the effect that indeed John Moyo had uttered the alleged words, which had been transcribed from a tape-recorder used at the rally and a tape of John Moyo's speech was duly played back.

After this, John Moyo was sworn, and the defence having had its examination-in-chief, he was cross-examined by the prosecutor.

'Do you admit you uttered the words you are alleged to have uttered at the rally?'

'Yes.'

'When you said the words in Count 1, what had you in mind?'

'I wanted to make a protest.'

'Why a protest?'

'Because the dogs looked vicious at the meeting where we were to discuss our rights and freedoms in this country.'

'You were aware that those were police dogs?'

'Yes. I protested at the very idea that dogs should be brought to our meeting especially to control us. Why should dogs control human gatherings?'

'You are supposed to answer and not to ask questions. I suggest to you that you said those words to expose the police dogs to ridicule, and indirectly the five dog handlers.'

After twenty minutes of close cross-examination, the prosecution proceeded to the next count.

'In Count 2, you are alleged to have said that the white

man rates his own humanity as 100 per cent; that of the Coloureds and Asians as 66⅔ per cent, and that of the black man as 33⅓ per cent. What did you mean by that?'

'What I meant was that the white man rates the black man in this country lowest.'

'Do you believe that?'

'Yes.'

'Don't you think this is because the African people as a whole are illiterate?'

'Educated or uneducated, their humanity is depreciated alike on no other grounds than that they are black.'

'Don't you think a statement like the one under which you are charged has the effect of causing Coloureds, Asians, and Africans to hate the whites here?'

'No, sir, I was trying to make the people there see the injustice inherent in the white man's scale of values, specially when it comes to the black man.'

'I put it to you, you were preaching hate?'

'No. I was preaching non-acceptance of racial inferiority. I was preaching a complete, unequivocal rejection of it.'

A stir ran through the courtroom.

'Now,' whispered one Son of the Soil to another, 'last year the white man sent Jeremiah Fambandoga to jail for telling a white girl how much he loved her. But today they want to send another Son of the Soil to jail because they suspect him of hating whites. You love them, jail. You hate them, jail. Either way, the black man in this country can't win. Either way, he must lose.'

On Count 3, the prosecution had proceeded, in cross-examination: 'You are alleged to have said that you must exterminate white supremacy root, stem, and branch. Correct?'

'Yes.'

'What section of the population believes in white supremacy?'

'The whites.'

'Are they the ones you were to exterminate root, stem, and branch?'

'No.'

'How were you going to exterminate white supremacy unless you exterminated the whites who you say believe in it?'

'White supremacy is an ideology, and it is the ideology that we desire exterminated.'

'I put it to you that by white supremacy you merely meant white people, and the people are likely to have interpreted it in that context?'

'No. There is a difference between an ideological system and people as people. The extermination of the former is not necessarily the extermination of the latter.'

'In Count 4, you assert that the Law and Order (Maintenance) Act is in fact a White Supremacy (Maintenance) Act. Correct?'

'Yes.'

'What did you mean by that?'

'Under the Law and Order (Maintenance) Act, the Minister may detain any person for political reasons for a maximum period of five years at a time. We have many political detainees in this country who have been in detention for over ten years now without any trial. Under the same Act, if political suspects are acquitted by any court of law, they may be sent into detention at the discretion of the Minister. Political prisoners upon their release, that is after serving their prison sentences, are sent into detention. As a matter of fact, we have over forty political prisoners who served their ten-year jail sentences but have now been served with detention orders, and they are now in detention at the pleasure of the Minister! The whole Act was designed to muzzle African political opinion so that white supremacy in this country may remain the order of the day for all time. This is why I call it the White Supremacy (Maintenance) Act because it was designed to maintain white supremacy in thought, word, and deed.'

'You say white supremacy was begotten of Satan. Correct?'

'Yes.'

'What do you mean?'

'I mean the evil spirit in the white man. It is this evil spirit in him which begot white supremacy.'

'Are you suggesting that the white man is not that evil spirit?'

'Rather, he is the embodiment of the evil spirit, but not necessarily it.'

'What do you mean?'

'That spirit has been cultivated in him, and it could be cultivated out of him, and a good spirit could be cultivated in him instead.'

'What do you mean by a good spirit?'

'An attitude of mind favourably disposed towards others.'

'Are you suggesting that the white man's attitude is not favourably disposed towards others?'

'White supremacy is an unfavourably disposed attitude of the mind of the white man towards non-whites.'

'In Count 5, you said courts are rubber-stamps of injustice. Correct?'

'Yes.'

'In what sense do you regard courts as rubber-stamps of injustice?'

'The courts do not make the law. They administer it. The law in this country is based on white supremacy, and therefore on injustice. The courts cannot alter this injustice already in the law. They must administer the law as it is. In other words, they must rubber-stamp the injustice in the law, and it is in this sense that I say courts are rubber-stamps of injustice.'

'In Count 6, you say magistrates and judges are servants of injustice. Correct?'

'Yes.'

'Are you aware that to label magistrates and judges as servants of injustice exposes them to ridicule and that this interferes with the administration of justice in this country?'

'I think it exposes them to truth, and this naturally strengthens the administration of justice. I can't see how exposure to truth can possibly interfere with the administration of justice.'

'Are you saying magistrates and judges live on injustice since they are paid for administering it?'

'Under the umbrella of white supremacy, yes, but under normal circumstances, no.'

'By normal circumstances, what do you mean?'

'I mean circumstances that are free from subjecting 95 per cent of the population to the interests of only 5 per cent of the same population. I mean a state of affairs wherein the laws of the country are based neither on white supremacy nor on black subjection, but on a square deal for all people regardless of the colour of their skin.'

John Moyo was then cross-examined on the next charge by the prosecution.

'In Count 7, you said, "The Chief Justice is in fact the Chief Injustice." Correct?'

'Yes.'

'What Chief Justice did you have in mind?'

'None.'

'But surely there can only be one Chief Justice in this country?'

'I had in mind the Chief Justice of this country as an institution, not as a person. I am not interested in fighting personal battles, but principles and institutions. Persons come and go, but institutions persist far beyond persons as individuals.'

'But surely since there's only one Chief Justice in this country, you expose him to ridicule and disaffection by calling him the Chief Injustice?'

'No, I expose the institution under white supremacy to legitimate criticism by the people whom it is supposed to serve.'

Eventually the prosecution moved on to the last charge.

'In Count 8, you say the police enforce injustice. Correct?'

'Yes.'

'What do you believe to be the functions of the police?'

'To prevent crime, to detect it, and to cause it to be punished.'

'How then do you reconcile that with what you say, that the police enforce injustice?'

'They have power to make neither just nor unjust laws, but they have power to enforce both kinds. Under white supremacy, they have power to enforce unjust laws, and therefore injustice.'

And so it came about in the end that on Counts 2, 3, 4, 5, 6, 7, and 8, John Moyo was acquitted, but he was found guilty on Count 1, and was sentenced to twelve months imprisonment without the option of a fine.

An appeal against conviction and sentence was noted to the High Court, and this would take anything between two to three months before the appeal would be heard. John Moyo was allowed bail of $500, and this gave him more time for his political organization.

10

Operation Dawn

Detective Inspector Harold Walker and Detective Inspector Cliff Briggs faced each other across a big writing-desk.

'There are strange things happening in the African townships these days,' began Walker.

'Yes, things have never been the same since that big rally,' agreed Briggs.

Both men were worried.

'Do you think it was what that witchdoctor said at the meeting which stirred it up?' asked Walker.

'Hard to say,' replied Briggs.

'Or do you think it's the killing of those thirty-five natives?'

'Could be.'

There was a knock on the door, and a black man carrying a stature of about six foot and a big round head with a round face lit up with a pair of white bright eyes appeared. As usual he was trembling, and his voice faltered here and there, and he looked uneasy in the presence of these two white men who were apparently his bosses. It was all part of politeness in the presence of the white man. It was a visible sign of his loyalty to them, and the white man took it as such.

'Yes, Johnnie, what's the score at Mabvuku?' asked Walker.

'Well, Mambo, everywhere I went the people are saying: "Stand firm!"'

' "Stand firm!" ' cried the two detectives almost in a duet.

'Yes, Mambo.'

'Where did you hear this?'

'At Mabvuku, Mambo.'

'I mean at what particular places?'

'Oh, in the beer hall, Mambo.'

'Where else?'

'At the school, Mambo.'

'School!'

'Yes, Mambo.'

'Where else?'

'At bus stops, Mambo.'

'Bus stops! Do you know what they meant when they said, "Stand firm!"?'

'No, Mambo.'

'Didn't you ask them?'

'No, Mambo.'

'Why not?'

'Because they would immediately suspect me.'

'You were quite right, Johnnie,' appreciated Detective Inspector Briggs. 'Who did you hear say those words?'

'At the school it was the headmaster, and then his pupils.'

'George Tafumaneyi?'

'Yes, Mambo.'

'But he's a government servant! Isn't he?'

'Oh, Mambo, government or not government servant, they are saying it.'

'What do you think they mean when they say, "Stand firm!"?'

'I don't know, Mambo.'

'I said what do *you think*?'

'Stand firm against the white man.'

'I see.'

'It's politics, Mambo. The whole township is politics. All bus stops are politics these days. All beer halls are politics. You hear politics everywhere, even in the lavatories, Mambo.'

'When they say, "Stand firm!", do they say anything else after that?'

'Yes, Mambo.'

'What?'

' "Action! Action! Action!" '

'Then after that, what do they do?'

'They lift their fists in the air and shout, "Black Power!" '

'Is it only men who do this?'

'No, Mambo. Women also. And boys and girls.'

'Have they all gone mad?'

'Yes, Mambo. All of them, young and old, have been bewitched.'

'By whom?'

'Dr John Moyo, Mambo.'

'He's the skelm!'

'Yes, Mambo.'

'Thank you, Johnnie, you can go. Listen carefully. Look carefully, and report here in two days time.'

'Yes, Mambo.' And with these words the black man removed his trembling, uneasy presence from the two detective inspectors, who had made sure not to give him a seat during the interview. Johnnie, who was in fact Tagwireyi Tarubinga, did not expect to be offered a chair so that he could sit down in the presence of the white men. He had been thoroughly drilled in his inferior status which he, like most blacks, had come to accept as a matter of course. White supremacy was to be dramatized in every situation that involved black and white.

'Well, what he says agrees with the reports we have here,' said Walker, pulling out a file.

'There can be no doubt that trouble is around the corner,' said Briggs.

Police reports from all over the country indicated clearly that the blacks were organizing themselves vigorously. The government had developed an efficient and extensive informer network in the townships, mining centres, mission schools, farms, Tribal Trust Lands, and any place where there was a sizeable concentration of blacks. Practically all African churches were infested with police informers and spies. A good number of blacks whose souls were made of hard cash and banknotes exploited European fears to their advantage. The whites on the white side of the wall sent these unscrupulous blacks to spy on their own oppressed people. As long as they could get money for informing and spying, as long as they could be patted on their backs by the white man for their foul deeds directed against their own people, and as long as they were able to buy themselves cars and radios, and drink themselves from sunrise to sunset, well, everything was fine for them, and the white man lost no chance of exploiting their greed for money, for women, for beer, and for material possessions. The unscrupulous blacks exploited the white man's fears of the emerging black political consciousness, and the unscrupulous white man exploited the black man's greed, his love of vanity, and his selfishness. Hence the white man cleverly used the black man to maintain white supremacy, and hence black subjection. In other words, the black man was made an effective tool of his own subjection. He was made to renounce his own birthright and to believe that he was indeed a third-rate citizen in his own country. This was why it was that he became an informer, a spy working against the collective interests of his own oppressed people. He had been told over and over again in his own country that he was, for practical purposes, a white man's tool, and no more. The white man's military planes had roared inside him, and the white man's guns deafened his ears so that before this apparently superior power he saw his own smallness, if not his own nothingness. He believed he was nothing, but he believed he could be something in the full service of white supremacy, and so he shuttled between the black and white sides of the wall, collected information from the black side in the name of Son and Daughter of the Soil, but delivered it wagging his tail on the white side for a chunk of meat thrown to him by the white man in acknowledgement of his many invaluable services to white supremacy.

But the blacks who were dedicated to a free Zimbabwe were also deeply concerned about what was going on on the white side of the wall. They therefore infiltrated the army, the police force, the prison service, and many other white-controlled undertakings. Even in the Special Branch of the Criminal Investigation Department they had their spies who kept them well informed on the goings-on on the white side of the wall. These blacks sharply felt that white supremacy had turned them into nothingness and as long as they remained under it, they would continue to be regarded as nothing. But deep down their hearts, to the very core of their being, they felt they were something. They rejected to be nothing in the land of their birth. But they could not be something while white supremacy held sway. It was imperative that they uprooted it in order to become something in their own country. This was the main purpose of their informer network on the white side of the wall.

Historically, black and white belonged together. Geographically, they belonged together. Economically, they also belonged together. But spiritually, ideologically, they were worlds apart. And each side kept its ear very close to the wall to hear what was going on on the other side.

Dan Shumba knocked respectfully on Detective Inspector Walker's door and came in.

'Now, Dan, what's all this about secret meetings of the P.P.?'

'Yes, Mambo. They are there all right.'

'Where?'

'In the townships, in the reserves.'

'Anywhere else?'

'Oh, Mambo, everywhere.'

'Where else specifically?'

'Mission schools, mines.'

'When do they hold these meetings?'

'At night, Mambo.'

'At about what time?'

'Oh, Mambo, at about ten.'

'And go on till about what time?'

'Up to about 1 a.m.'

'What are they trying to do?'

'Well, Mambo, they are planning.'

'Planning to do what?'

Dan Shumba went closer to the desk; but for it, he would have moved even closer. He lowered his voice, and, almost in a whisper, he said, 'I think they are planning to massacre all the whites.'

'When?'

'I don't know.'

'Where?'

'Everywhere.'

'Soon?'

'I don't think so. Maybe a month, two months.'

'Why do you think they have put it off so far?'

'I think they want to do a thorough job of it. This is why they are holding meetings all over the country and late at night.'

'But if they kill all the whites, how will they be able to get on without them?'

'Well, their argument is that the black man was in this country before the white man came here.'

'Look, Dan. Do you think they record the proceedings of these meetings?'

'Naturally.'

'Thank you, Dan. You can go. Keep your ears open. Keep your eyes open, the government will richly reward you.'

'Thank you, Mambo.'

'Well, as we thought, there's going to be real trouble. The blacks are planning to massacre all the whites in this country,' said Walker.

'It makes a great deal of sense to me,' remarked Briggs.

'To me too,' admitted Walker. 'The political arithmetic now adds up right. "Stand firm!" can only mean that the blacks must stand firm when we strike back as they try to execute this hideous plan of theirs.'

In three days time the police raided the houses of all the officials of the People's Party. This included all the national, provincial, district, and branch officials throughout the country. The police collected as many handwritten and typed documents as they could, and took them to their various stations for close examination. The minute books were also among such documents. The documents they were looking for were those relating to the alleged massacre plot. Any piece of paper that hinted at that was to be sent to the police headquarters at Salisbury. Fort Victoria, Umtali, Gwelo, Bulawayo, and other centres like Gatooma, Que Que, Sinoia, and Wankie reported in a matter of four days of hard work often going well into the night that no data relating to the alleged plot had been unearthed. Salisbury was also in the same position.

Dan Shumba had thought that the police seizure of the various documents of the People's Party throughout the country was going to establish his claim of a massacre plot. He had sincerely believed that something of that nature would be discovered, and this would naturally reflect creditably upon him, and assure him of his continuity on the payroll of white supremacy. But he was deeply disappointed when all the reports were negative. He was paid as a police spy $75 per month which was considered a little too high for a black man, but since the white man needed information from the black side of the wall, and since Dan Shumba knew how to collect it, having the gift of the gab and speaking English, Shona, Ndebele, and Nyanja well, and dined, wined, and womanized easily and thus made more contacts than most people, it was thought worthwhile to pay him that much. But the massacre plot had not been substantiated by any documentary evidence, and Shumba naturally felt that his $75 might slip through his fingers. So he stumbled on a brilliant idea, and smiled to himself for the versatility of his genius or ingenuity. He forged a letter to Dr John Moyo and signed it Josiah Gabaza. He drove to Bulawayo by night and returned to Salisbury about 4 a.m.

Three days later Shumba was called to the C.I.D. office in Salisbury.

'Dan,' began Detective Inspector Walker, 'I don't know

what I would do without you. The massacre plot is true after all. Look at this.'

Dan Shumba read the letter:

> 1678/90 Mpopoma
> Mpopoma Township
> Bulawayo
> 2 June

Dear Dr Moyo,

I would advise that in future we do not have any minutes written up for these special meetings we are having these days. There must not be even a scrap of paper written about anything we say there. If our men in enemy ranks had not advised us of the raid, that master plan would have been captured. I would also advise that you destroy the one in the cave. I hope they found nothing incriminating on you.

Stand firm, Son of the Soil.

> Yours in the Struggle,
> Josiah Gabaza

'Now, Dan, call again around here at 3 this afternoon.'

'Yes, Mambo,' said Dan obediently, and left.

'Dan must be pleased that his report is nearly correct,' commented Briggs. 'But I've been wondering. Could it possibly be that an enemy of the witchdoctor wrote that letter?'

'It's possible, Cliff. These African nationalists are always squabbling among themselves for positions. But the tone of the letter is that of a loyal colleague who accepts his leadership without any doubt. And again this letter is postmarked Bulawayo. I think it's genuine advice from a P.P. man.'

The two detectives pieced together the various pieces of information at their disposal. They were satisfied with the whole chain of events, and that it would be acceptable to higher authority as a factual report on which they could reasonably take action. Hence, on the white side of the wall, 'Stand firm!' was taken to mean the massacre of whites in some immediate future, but on the black side it had only one meaning, and that was to stand firm against police provocation and intimidation as had been experienced at the big rally. 'Stand firm!' meant in effect, 'Don't be frightened by police intimidation!' It meant that all the supporters of the

People's Party should remain unflinching, inflexible, and determined. They must stand firm by their cause of black
liberation. Briefly, on the black side of the wall the message
was LIBERATION, but on the white side it was construed
to be WHITE MASSACRE; and Dan Shumba, the callous,
unscrupulous black spy whose soul was not sensitive to anything else except money and a vision of the well-to-do man,
was responsible for this definition of 'Stand firm!' on the
white side of the wall.

Four days later, exactly at 12 midnight, police and police
reservists supported by the army gathered at the police
station in each district. There were police and army trucks.
At 1 a.m. each commanding officer in each district gave
identical orders to his men to close in on suspected houses in
the townships and in the rural areas, and to raid them at
4 a.m. During the day the suspects had been trailed by detectives in plain clothes who kept in constant touch with the
police headquarters. Exactly at 3 a.m. the police raids began
right throughout the country; about 1,270 men and youths
were collected into the police and army trucks and by 5.30
a.m. most of these were in police custody. All the leading
members of the People's Party had been arrested and were
understood to be concentrated in Salisbury, Gwelo, and
Khami prisons. The big haul included all the members of the
Central Committee, the provincial, district, and branch
officials. On the white side of the wall there was great relief
and even satisfaction, but on the black side there was great
frustration and anxiety.

The joys of the white side were the unhappiness of the
black side, and the fears of the former were the contentment
of the latter, and it could not be otherwise in such a country.
Operation Dawn had not solved the problem. It had only
suppressed it. What is suppressed has a tendency to spring
back to normal as circumstances allow. The white side, however, rejoiced at Operation Dawn, because they could not dis-
tinguish under the blinding glare and the deafening roar of
white supremacy between solving and suppressing a problem.

11

On the Precipice's Edge

'I can't believe it,' said Mrs Ida Moswa of Mrewa district, Mashonaland. 'They just burst into our bedroom, and literally pulled him out of bed. Oh, these people, these people.'

'Exactly what they did to us!' corroborated Mrs Mary Pasindoga. 'They rushed into our bedroom, and before I knew what it was all about, I was left alone. He was gone in his pyjamas, just like that!'

'These people are *mhuka chaidzo*, real animals,' said Ida Moswa.

'Not even *Mwari*, God Himself, would have done such a thing,' suggested Mary Pasindoga.

'A man in bed with his wife, and in they come unceremoniously tearing him away from his wife's arms! Ah . . . these people . . . these people . . . real animals,' mourned Ida Moswa.

'Do these animals really know the privacy of other people's bedrooms?' wondered Mary Pasindoga.

'Do they know the intimacy of privacy?'

'I wonder, Mrs Moswa!'

'Unbelievable! Unbelievable!' Ida Moswa cried.

'The real trouble is that they don't think we are people. They think we are animals,' said Mary Pasindoga.

'You are right.'

'If they thought we were people like themselves, they wouldn't treat us like that.'

'And they have actually tamed our men, you know?'

'Yes. They've castrated them.'

'Their bullets have castrated them, but why can't our men get bullets so that they can also behave like men instead of being treated like this by other men like themselves?'

The two black women commiserated with each other for nearly two hours. Their husbands had gone. Where? They did not know. The only thing they knew was that their husbands had been taken away by armed police and shoved into police trucks at the crack of dawn, and that the trucks had disappeared from the scene, and that their sounds had died in the distance. The police would not tell them where they were taking their husbands. For the next two months many wives and other relatives did not know the whereabouts of their beloved ones. They moved from jail to jail according to the strength of rumours in search of their beloved ones who had temporarily disappeared into the belly of white supremacy where they were supposed to be regenerated into finer men obedient to the whims of the white man. The two women, like so many others, had two problems to solve: where and when to see their beloved ones. The children had the same problems. The two women, like so many others, had now seen white supremacy in their own bedrooms! They now knew what it meant to be ruled by foreigners. They never forgot it. They now knew that white supremacy burst into a man's bedroom, humiliated him in the presence of his own wife, the queen of his heart, kicked or rudely pushed him out of his bedroom and out of his house, and then just shoved him into the police trucks. Operation Dawn had been more eloquent than many of Dr Moyo's most brilliant speeches.

In the Essexvale district, Matebeleland, the reaction to Operation Dawn was very bitter, and women there, as in the rest of the country, shared their sorrow with one another.

'Oh, daughter of Duke,' said Mrs Jessie Hlazo, 'you don't know what happened to us. Even a very angry and bad father would not pull out of bed his own naked two-year-old son as they did my husband. I pray I shall never again see my husband humiliated like that by other men like himself. Oh, those dogs!'

'Dogs indeed! And what can we expect from dogs?' asked Mrs Ntombizodwa Ndebele, still shocked by the police raid.

'They have been breast-fed on disrespect and rudeness,' cursed Jessie Hlazo.

'They have been brought up in the tradition of oppressing and humiliating black people. They would feel less than themselves if they did not do so,' said Ntombizodwa Ndebele.

'I don't know why God should have made me a woman! I would have taught those dogs a good lesson,' pined Jessie Hlazo.

Operation Dawn had left bitterness behind its trail. The young people who had escaped the police dragnet were very bitter, and they accused their elders of downright cowardice. They did not spare John Moyo. They flayed him alive with their venom-charged militant tongues.

The various Rhodesian jails received various groups of political detainees most of whom were to remain there for the next five years renewable thereafter for another five years if the detainee in question did not show evidence that he had repented of his errors. They had been detained without trial, and they had been detained at the Minister's pleasure, and this made their situation worse since the Minister was a politician, and they his political rivals, and he had suddenly clipped their wings in the interest of his own political survival. The detainees wondered how their families could get to know where they were. They had been flatly told that for the next two months they would not be allowed to write or receive any letter. Between them and the outside world there was to be absolute blankness. No visitor would be allowed to see them during that period. They were promised, however, that after that time this position would be reviewed.

Operation Dawn also caused a great deal of excitement and discussion on the white side of the wall. The local newspapers carried the story of the massacre plot, and the whites were relieved that it had been nipped in the bud. They were full of praises for the efficiency of the police force. Most of them felt the problem of the black threat had been effectively dealt with. With more than a thousand black nationalists in the safe custody of the prisons they felt the lesson had been driven home to the people on the black side of the wall, and the lesson they hoped had been hammered into their heads was that it did not pay to oppose the white man.

'I wonder how the witchdoctor is faring in prison!' said Jerry Cary with an unmistakable cynical smile and with his eyes twinkling with evil but delicious mischief. 'That's where he should have been locked up eighteen months ago!'

The four white men who were drinking with him chorussed their agreement.

'I hope he's now consulting his bones to know when he's coming out to make more trouble for the white man,' laughed Cary.

'But in fact the veneer of the white man's education had gone to his head,' asserted Nicholas Fletcher seriously.

'Of course it had,' agreed Cary with deep satisfaction.

'The witchdoctor had come to believe that he was an equal of the white man,' observed Leslie Jones.

'I wonder what his followers will do without him,' asked Fletcher.

'If another witchdoctor raises his head, why, of course his proper place is behind iron bars,' answered Cary. 'There can be no compromise whatsoever. Every nigger must be made to understand that this is a white man's country. This is not another Zambia or Tanzania. Niggers who want to rule must cross the Zambezi.'

'The police have been extremely efficient,' said Peter Potter. 'They collected all the black agitators just like that! They couldn't have done it better.'

'No. Excellent piece of work. Even the clever witchdoctor must be surprised behind the iron bars,' said Cary.

'His bones should have told him that trouble was on the way.'

All the five men laughed boisterously. They filled their glasses with Castle beer.

'To the good health of our clever witchdoctor!' toasted Cary.

'And may he prosper behind the iron bars!' proposed Fletcher, and all five laughed, holding their glasses of beer in their hands waiting for every one of them to say something.

'And may he rule behind the iron bars according to majority rule!' proposed Henry Slater.

They all laughed, and in a big chorus they toasted, 'To the clever witchdoctor!' and clicked their glasses, and then drained their absolute pleasure down their alimentary canals. Their sense of horse-play centred around Operation Dawn until they filled again their glasses.

'To the Sons of the Soil behind the iron bars!' toasted Cary.

'May they liberate their Soil behind the iron bars!' proposed Fletcher.

'May they never be buried in their Soil behind the iron bars!' proposed Jones.

'May they never soil the prison premises!' proposed Slater.

'To the Sons of the Soil and their iron bars!' they all toasted, and let beer wash down their contentment to mingle with their very being.

'One thing which I cannot understand is how all these niggers have allowed one nigger to put them into trouble like this,' reflected Jones.

'Niggers will always be niggers, you know. They can't and they won't think,' replied Cary.

'The only thing a nigger knows is to have too many concubines, and then breed like rabbits,' said Potter.

'Woman-shooting is every nigger's main occupation. They can't fight like the white man,' said Slater.

'Oh, the monkeys have no guts to fight,' added Cary. 'The only thing they know is talk, talk, and ape the white man.'

'Get them to fight one another, why, they will even tear

one another with their savage teeth, but get them to fight the white man, of course they will always turn tail,' said Slater.

'But,' objected Jones, 'they are learning to stand up against the white man. I'm not too happy with what has happened in the Zambezi Valley. The niggers actually killed white men with the white man's guns!'

'Oh, but that's an exception,' objected Cary. 'That's not the common run of niggers.'

'But I'm afraid that with the Soviet Union and China supporting these niggers the exception will soon prove to be the rule unless we're very careful.'

'And that's why Operation Dawn is so commendable,' stressed Cary. 'The niggers must never be allowed to reach a position when they would challenge the white man on a battlefield. The government must tighten up on who goes out of this country and who goes where.'

'What time do you make it, Henry?' asked Cary.

'Nine.'

'Let's hear what Zambia has to say today. Those niggers are just mad against us. Tune in, will you.'

The five men listened keenly. The Zambia programme had just begun.

'. . . It is your duty, Sons and Daughters of Zimbabwe, to come here and join us so that we may train so that we can re-trieve our stolen Fatherland. We are our own liberators. No one will liberate us but ourselves. History is on the side of the black man, and the white man in Rhodesia is fighting a losing battle.

'Since our arrival here two days ago I have been greatly encouraged by the moral and material support that other countries are giving us. They are all ready to give us the tools, but we must be ready to do the job ourselves! No one will do the job for us but ourselves. We are the key to our own freedom and independence.

'We must be prepared to meet force with force. We intend to match bullet power with bullet power. It has to be a full-fledged armed struggle if we are to be our own liberators.

'Once more, I say to you, Sons and Daughters of Zimbabwe: we are our own liberators. Good night.'

Then immediately the voice of the announcer was heard: 'That was Dr John Moyo speaking to the people of Zimbabwe. He and his three colleagues escaped a police dragnet in Rhodesia two days ago. He will again be on the air on Friday at the same time.'

'Wha . . . wha . . . wha . . . what?' stammered Cary. 'He escaped!'

'Incredible!' cried Slater.

'I can't believe it!' exclaimed an outraged Jones.

'It can't be true!' said Potter, utterly disgusted.

'Of all the . . .,' choked Fletcher.

'Operation Dawn wasted!' lamented Slater. 'The witch-doctor was the real target.'

'You feel you've captured a cheetah, just to find you've only captured his tail, and he's gone!' cried Cary. 'You feel you've captured a leopard, just to find you've only captured his tail, and he's gone! You feel you've captured a tiger, just to find you've only captured his tail, and he's gone! You feel you've captured a lion, just to find you've captured his tail, and he's gone! That's what has happened here, and what good are these tails to the white man? The problem is far from being solved, no matter how many tails we may put behind the iron bars!'

'It's the head that must be captured,' said Jones.

To these five men the hundreds of black politicians who had been collected and placed behind the iron bars literally became tails and John Moyo became the many dangerous animals that had escaped the police dragnet, minus their tails of course! The police swoop lost most of its significance when it was finally learnt that John Moyo had found his way into friendly Zambia with three other members of his Central Committee. On the white side of the wall therefore the news of John Moyo's escape was received with shock, disgust, and indignation!

On the black side of the wall, however, the reception was

quite different. The black radio listeners had heard the news in Shona, Ndebele, and English. They were extremely happy that John Moyo and three of his lieutenants had clean escaped the police dragnet. They knew his dedication and devotion to the cause of the black man. They knew his enormous energies. They knew he never spared himself when the cause of the black man was involved. They were confident that he was now going to work even harder than before. He was their ray of hope, and even those detained P.P. men cheered with their fisted hands when some equally delighted jail guards passed on to them this most encouraging piece of news. They thanked and blessed their ancestral spirits that the Son of the Soil had found his way to Zambia. The four firebrands—Silas Mushonga, Simon Mugadza, John Sibanda, and Gideon Masuku—who had escaped the police swoop, were still in Salisbury, where they carried on with their work as usual. They were jubilant that John Moyo and at least three others were safe in Zambia.

'That was the best news since the police raid,' remarked Gideon Masuku, switching off the radio.

'The Son of the Soil will now have his eyes wide open because he'll be surrounded by other black revolutionaries,' said Silas Mushonga.

'This will do him a lot of good,' said John Sibanda.

'Ah, the spirits of our ancestors are still with us,' Gideon Masuku said thankfully. 'Oh, may they help and guide him!'

'He needs all their support,' remarked Simon Mugadza.

'Now the struggle for the liberation of our country will take a more interesting turn. It won't be a talking struggle, but a shooting one, and then the white man will understand us better,' said Silas Mushonga.

'I really liked what the Son of the Soil said over the radio. He said we must meet force with force. That's good, Sons of the Soil. That's man's language. That's realism. That's the way to look at it,' said Simon Mugadza.

'That was really good,' the other three agreed.

'Did you hear him? He said: "We are our own liberators," '

asked Silas Mushonga. 'From now on we must tell everyone
that our motto is, "We are our own liberators!" Every driver,
teacher, student, farmer, worker, man, woman, boy, and
girl must repeat this three times a day—in the morning, at
midday, and at night.'

'That would be wonderful.'

'I really mean it. I'm serious. As people pass one another
let them whisper: "We are our own liberators!" '

'It's a good idea.'

'This we can easily put across. Our machinery is efficient.'

'In a week's time the motto should be repeated everywhere in the country,' said Gideon Masuku.

'But the Son of the Soil wants men across so that they may
be trained to fight. To *fight*! Ah! I like that word, you know.
It warms up my blood, and I would wring the neck of a
white man in no time,' asserted Silas Mushonga. 'Nothing
could be nobler than to fight for our own rights; to bleed for
them; to groan for them on the battlefield; and finally to pay
the supreme price for them. That's to be men, Sons of the
Soil!'

The four firebrands then drew up plans of quietly recruit-
ing more men to go for military training in order to meet the
challenge on equal terms with the white man. The response
was good since more men were leaving the country practically every week to be sent to the Soviet Union, China, Cuba,
Algeria, Egypt, Ghana, and Tanzania.

The whites on the white side of the wall became more and
more apprehensive when information reached them about
the young blacks leaving the country for military training,
and that sooner or later these would return as invaders. The
Government declared a state of emergency, posted soldiers
along the borders, and got planes ready to blast out the Sons
of the Soil who were determined to retrieve their stolen land.
Hence Rhodesia became encircled as it were by a wall of
white supremacy through which the black militants were
determined to break, but which white militants were also
determined to protect. There were only two ways of breaking

this wall, namely by democratic means—but the whites almost to a man had rejected this—or by means of force—and the blacks had no choice but to adopt this.

The ideology of white supremacy, based on the subjection of the black man in Rhodesia, denied the black man his full fundamental human rights and freedoms in his own native land and built a wall between black and white. The blacks decided, as the last resort, that they were going to shoot down this wall; but the whites decided that this wall was to be maintained at any cost in spite of the glaring injustices inherent in it.

Hence the whole country—a beautiful country from Nature's hand, but despoiled and embittered by white intransigence—was brought to the precipice's edge. But there grew the ROOTS OF A REVOLUTION.

48004638

PR 9390 .9 .S5R75 1977

SITHOLE   NDABANINGI.

ROOTS OF A
REVOLUTION   SCENES

**MONTGOMERY COLLEGE
LIBRARY**

Rockville Campus

MONTGOMERY COLLEGE LIBRARY
GERMANTOWN CAMPUS

MONTGOMERY COLLEGE LIBRARIES
PR 9390.9.S5R751977
Roots of a re

germ. circ

0 0000 00181215 5